BRAIN FITNESS
Breakthrough Training
for Those Who Mind

BRAIN FITNESS
Breakthrough Training
for Those Who Mind

Ann J. Polya, Ph.D.

To order additional copies of this book, contact:
Xlibris Corporation
1-888-795-4274
www.Xlibris.com
Orders@Xlibris.com
60176

Contents

PART TWO: BREAKTHROUGH TRAINING
AND BRAIN FITNESS

Acknowledgements

I would like to thank my friends and family for all their support and encouragement they have given me over this journey.

Thanks, in particular to JoAnn Bock and Doug Ramsey, for their helpful suggestions for the book, its cover and promotion. Also special thanks to Lynn Hearn, Elsie Bickford and JoAnn Bock for their valuable feedback on the sessions I have given at Lost Tree Village, North Palm Beach, Florida.

Thanks also to Amy Arnsten Ph.D., Kevin Ochsner Ph.D., and Lila Devachi, Ph.D. for the inspiration of their work in Neuroscience.

Finally my thanks also go to Kuma and Winston for their devotion and their special four-legged loyalty.

Preface

The New Paradigm—as applied to Brain Fitness.

As the twenty first century moves towards its second decade, the search for mechanical perfection that prevailed until recently is beginning to fade in favor of the new paradigm of functionality. We are experiencing a paradigm shift, a term first used by Thomas Kuhn in 1960, who considered that no two paradigms could co-exist, and a shift would occur from the prevailing paradigm when there were changes to basic assumptions and views on reality. This appears to be happening now.

The aim of the previous paradigm was to make things bigger, better and faster, and with a more efficient structure. This now-dated paradigm reflected a quest for excellence and encouraged consumers to view medicine and its products as reliable cures to fix anything—including aging. The new approach is an acceptance that things do not have to be perfect, and the new aim is to make things work, establish how and in what way, and accept the need to adapt to circumstances rather than insist on infallibility.

This change, predicted by Arnold Brown in the 2008 Futurist, is sweeping all forms of science. It encompasses the shift towards a focus on our strengths rather than remediation of our weaknesses in the hope of becoming a perfect performer. It reflects Apple's concept of renting music using their iTunes. In terms of Brain Fitness, this pragmatic approach no longer relies on fix-the-weakness, but gives us strategies to build on what we can do in order to achieve our goals and choose how we want to operate. Consequently, the aim no longer is to pretend that age can be remediated by surgery or injections, but establish how we can perform well and improve our life span.

This new matter-of-fact quest for what works accompanies advances in Neuroscience on the nature of our brains. In the last fifteen years, we have learned that our brains can grow throughout our lives. Out is the old paradigm, and former conventional view, that our brains develop to their maximum by early adulthood and thereafter the brain's structure is "fixed" and will decline with age or degenerative loss. New research shows that our brains are not "hardwired" in childhood, but the adult brain can grow and change its structure and function throughout our lives.

This pragmatic new paradigm also applies to the Behavioral Sciences. It permits the formation of Behavioral Breakthrough Training which is a fresh way of looking at our processes of thinking and feeling and ways in which we can effectively bring about changes that work for us. This Breakthrough Training consists of a range of techniques and tools that concentrate on what works well and effectively to boost our Brain Fitness.

Within this palette for effective change, Breakthrough Training is able to apply the behavioral tools of cognitive and dialectical techniques to a much wider audience than at their origins; these can assist us all with the review and ways to alter our thinking and emotive responses capably and effectively. Additionally Breakthrough Training uses Emotional Intelligence tools that help establish the validity of our feelings and thoughts, and provide ways to modify selective ones that will improve our Emotional Intelligence ratings and help us operate effectively and intelligently from a cognitive and emotive perspective. Also included are other valuable techniques used in Meditation, Visualization, and personal balance and self-care.

When we are effective we also gain more direct sway over the feelings and the thoughts we express, which impacts our behavior and also the levels of chemicals released in our brains; this further impacts our mood and also can trigger or halt the production of a brain chemical that is crucial for Neuroplasticity, or the malleability of our brains. It is this plasticity that can make changes, including behavioral changes provoked by Breakthrough Training, sustainable or more endurable.

The concept of Brain Fitness, used in this book, is a dynamic one that includes both our cognitive abilities and the advances of Neuroscience; the former being our thoughts and emotions—including our memory, communication skills, focus and our decision-making abilities, and the latter includes the knowledge that we can grow new brain cells via Neurogenesis, and that these new cells and pathways can adapt and be malleable via Neuroplasticity. Both these aspects interface with each other, and we have the ability to capitalize on our new knowledge of our brains as well as our option to use Breakthrough Training with its techniques to bolster control over our thoughts and emotions so that we attain our goals.

In this Brain Fitness program the tools are introduced and explained to facilitate our own "do-it-yourself" change. We can learn new ways to function with adaptability and alter our actions; this in turn impacts the functioning of our brains. It is this aspect of the new paradigm that eminent scientist, Freeman Dyson, calls the "biology century" because our focus is creating a functional approach in the way that nature adapts to its environment and circumstances.

In fact, as I prepared for a series of workshops on "Brain Fitness" given in North Palm Beach, Florida in early 2009, I was constantly reminded of the saying—you can't teach an "old dog new tricks", but in fact you can! We now know that our brains are not like old machines with built-in obsolescence but they are adaptable and pliable tools that can be changed by our choice, irrespective of age or genetics.

This book will focus on how our brains work, the impact of Neurogenesis and Neuroplasticity, our abilities to think and feel and our use of Breakthrough Training to modify these patterns. Brain Fitness is the sum of all of these changes; it can add significant benefits that range from better memories, attention, problem solving and spatial processing and counteract, and in part even reverse, the impact of aging. All we have to do is choose to follow our Brain Fitness Program.

Part One

Brain Fitness and Neuroscience

Chapter One

Brain Fitness in the 21st century

"Nothing great was ever achieved without enthusiasm"—
Ralph Waldo Emerson

Our brains are responsible for most of the things we care about—language, imagination, logic, empathy, creativity and how we make ethical decisions. Yes, we do need our other organs to keep alive, but how often do we remember that our brains are vital to our very essence. Our brains are where we store all the feelings and emotions we have ever experienced, and contain all thoughts and thinking "software" to process and analyze new and old facts.

Brain Fitness

Brain Fitness consists of a set of tools that can help us improve the way our brains function, empower us to positively influence our thoughts and emotions, and can help us slow the normal aging process. We now know that there are complex options to direct new growth of brain cells and pathways into certain activities. Through advances in Neuroscience we have a better understanding of how the brain works, and how we might be able to induce changes. Additionally we know that that our thoughts and feelings impinge on the brain through the levels of certain key chemicals produced, notably Norepinephrine and Dopamine, which can trigger a brain growth chemical that can change our brain circuitry as well as prompt physical actions.

This Brain Fitness program is based on developments in Neurosciences and Behavioral techniques, and is a functional "do-it-yourself" program. With this program we can construct behavioral approaches that enable Breakthrough Training to boost our true wellbeing by increasing our memory, problem-solving ability, empathy and our savoir-faire and personal satisfaction; moreover, these changes can endure via the use of Neuroplasticity.

Road to aging has a detour

Until fairly recently, conventional wisdom held that the brain was fixed with a definitive structure and anatomy, which stops its development after an initial phase that ends in late childhood. Studies now show that the brain is not "hardwired" in childhood, and we are not limited by our genetic heritage or DNA. To the contrary, our brains are pliable, elastic and changeable throughout our lives-irrespective of our age or genetics. However, we must choose to bring about changes that boost our awareness, our thinking capacities, and counteract issues arising from the normal aging process.

It is only in the 21st century we have learned that we can capitalize on the advances in Brain Science to modify our "fate", and slow or even reverse the effects of aging. Indeed we have the power to take more control over our thoughts, feelings and actions, and thereby influence our brain circuitry along the lines we prefer. This power depends on our choice and how we opt to deploy our own resources.

Neurogenesis

Neuroscience studies show that brain cells, or neurons, can and do grow. This is called Neurogenesis. This was a major advance in Neuroscience, or the science of the brain. It came after intense examination of our brains cells, or neurons, which are unlike the other cells in our bodies that divide and re-grow as, for instance, happens in the case for skin in the healing of a cut. Scientists established that we are able to grow new neurons, and our brains also can strengthen the colossal number of pathways and connections between neurons. This advance, Neurogenesis, proves that any adult brain is not like a hardwired machine but can expand and change.

Neuroplasticity

Not only can we create new brain cells, or Neurogenesis, but we can also do so in ways that change how our brain's function and their structures. Indeed these neurons are capable of restructuring our brain circuits, and can be reprogrammed and grow new or stronger connections between each neuron. This is called Neuroplasticity as it means that we can direct our brains to be more plastic or malleable, and thereby more adaptable to change according to circumstances and environments. This Neuroplasticity can happen throughout our lives.

In our early years the brain sets up a type of learning system that when we experience a noise, sight or sound, these are translated into impulses understood by our brains and passed along the brain's pathways—or neuron routes. As more data is imputed in childhood, it is refined by the brain and creates more complex pathways for greater control. Neurons are stimulated directly through experience, which can be real or imagined, or indirectly through these connections from neighboring neurons. Neuroplasticity, or brain malleability, allows the brain's estimated 100 billion nerve cells, to constantly lay down new pathways for neural communication, and rearrange existing ones throughout life; this aids the processes of learning, memory, and adaptation through experience.

This plasticity is impacted by our thoughts and feelings. Consequently we can incite activity of our brain cells and their connections with neighboring neurons for functional and structural malleability through our conscious thinking. Hence, if we so decide, we can choose to change our brains for self-improvement as Sharon Begley underscores in her 2007 book.

Without the ability to make such functional changes, our brains would not be able to memorize a new fact, master a new skill, form a new memory or adjust to a new environment; nor would we be able to recover from brain injuries or overcome cognitive disabilities. Moreover, without Neuroplasticity we would not be able to benefit from a Brain Fitness program.

Technological advances

Brain imaging has been made possible by an array of machines that now allow us to see "inside" the brain. There are different types of brain imaging machines; both structural and functional.

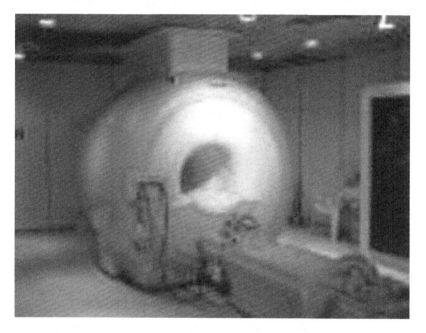

CT scanner

Structural imaging reveals data about the shape and volume of the brain and use CT and MRI scans; which take large numbers of two-dimensional X-rays images that are used to digitally compute 3D images of the inside of the brain. Functional imaging shows the brain cells that are active when we perform a specific task (fMRI and PET scans).

We now are able to show, in real time, a Neuro-image of the impact of complex human feelings and thoughts on the brain, and track how they affect different parts of the brain by the production and release of certain chemicals in our brain circuitry.

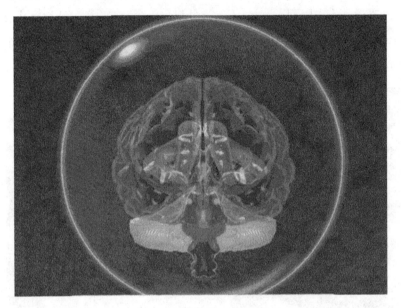

Image of our Brain

These technological advances enable real time observation of Neurogenesis and Neuroplasticity in action. This has revolutionized our ability to study the human brain as we can immediately see whether something works or not and thereby assists our ability to track changes as the brain adapts and alters its structure to meet changing circumstances.

Tools for Neuroplasticity

With Neurogenesis, we are able to grow new cells or neurons, and studies show that we are able to boost our brain circuitry with better and stronger connections between neurons and our brain's ability to develop more branches among neurons that ramps up the volume and thickness.

Not only do we want to encourage growth, but we also want to use the plasticity of growing new cells to make positive adaptations, or positive Neuroplasticity. What do we need to do for this to happen? Studies indicate that stimulated or enhanced brains are more likely to grow new brain cells.

Stimulation of the Brain

There is evidence that the key triggers for the stimulation of the brain are:-

- Physical activities
- Mental activities
- Social engagements

In particular, all evidence points to the fact that "appropriate" physical activities are the single most important stimulating factor. This is followed stimulation from specific types of mental or intellectual activities and thirdly that we also need some socializing stimulation as evidence indicates the harmful effects of isolation on the brain's ability for growth.

Novelty and Challenge

For all forms of brain stimulation we need activities that are increasingly testing. We can do this by incorporating new elements and also by including more challenging steps with greater difficulty levels. These factors are essential to Brain stimulation and for its ability to grow and stay healthy. Our brains can learn new things at any age and are much adept at doing so when the steps are progressive and the challenge and novelty are real and incremental.

"Use it or Lose it"

As with physical fitness, if we do not continue to work out, we begin to lose our form. In the same way with Brain Fitness, we need to keep using it, otherwise we will lose it. This can happen throughout our lives. To best capitalize on our brain's potential, we are well advised to continue with some form of stimulation to maintain Brain Fitness; so if we have some form of impediment, such as a physical injury, we need to keep up with some minimum physical exercise, but ensure that we factor in compensation by using increased intellectual challenges or social engagements.

Three activities that stimulate Neuroplasticity:-

A.   Exercise

We all know that physical exercise helps us feel better since it pumps more blood to our brain cells so they function better, and it helps us deal with anxieties and muscle tensions. We also know that we are born movers, and the modern more sedentary lifestyle is linked to the facts that 65% of US adults are overweight or obese, and 10% have Diabetes-type two.

Yet what is relatively new is the knowledge that adequate and appropriate physical exercise actually is good for our brains too. It boosts our chemical production that helps neurons grow and stay healthy; in other words it helps our brains grow.

Most research began using experiments with animals, as did the work at the University of British Columbia in 2004, which showed certain types of physical exercise in animals induced changes in the brain by the production of complex dendrites, or bushy projections, that enable a neuron to receive signals from other neurons. These allow the brain to gather more facts, retrieve memories and see the links between facts and enhance learning.

Physical exercise does not make us smart, but it helps our brains by setting in motion our readiness to change. It is a pre-condition for Neuroplasticity that will affect our moods, attention, ability to learn and can reverse some effects of aging in the brain. The act of exercising can boost our levels of chemicals, notably Norepinephrine and Dopamine that trigger the production of another major Neuroplasticity inducing chemical.

We know that reduced levels of these naturally occurring chemicals, Norepinephrine and Dopamine, in our systems are linked to boring surroundings and lack of exercise; and often manifest as Attention Deficit Disorder (ADD), impulsivity, lack of concentration, depression and loss of pleasure. On the other hand, high levels of Dopamine add to a feeling of pleasure and are sometimes imitated by substances such as cocaine, heroin, cigarettes, coffee and alcohol, which can lead to addictions.

Reasonable levels of Norepinephrine and Dopamine can lower stress, anxiety and tension, and significantly promote Neuroplasticity by triggering the production of BDNF or Brain-derived neurotrophic factor that is essential for Neuroplasticity. This increase in BDNF production acts as a charge for Neuroplasticity and enables our brains to grow and strengthen the pathways connecting these neurons.

Exercise helps our physical well-being by preventing accretion of weight, and aids our cardiovascular readings. It also elevates our stress thresholds, lifts our moods, boosts our immune system and helps us balance our diet so we are less likely to develop diabetes. This extra amount of BDNF produced by exercise is approximately equivalent to that induced by the use of many of the anti-depressants on the market. This puts us in driver's seat to manage our brain's processes of what and how we cope with life's daily challenges, and frees us from feelings of helplessness and guilt.

This physical exercise—more than any of the three possible options—has the biggest impact on instigating increased Neuroplastic activity and all the consequent benefits.

BDNF or Brain-derived neurotrophic factor

With technological advances, we now know more about the action of BDNF, or Brain-derived neurotrophic factor, on our human brain. Examination of the impact of exercise by scientists shows the effect starts in our muscles, which when contracted transmit more protein IGF-1 via the bloodstream to our brains, and this sets off an increased production of BDNF, or Brain-derived neurotrophic factor; the extra BDNF boosts our neuronal activity and helps the growth of new neurons and strengthening of the connections between them.

Growth and Strengthening
Effect of BDNF

The additional production of BDNF promotes the survival of existing neurons and encourages the growth and differentiation of new neurons and their synapses which are all vital for learning, memory, and higher thinking. This is a major active component in our brains that we need to spur Neurogenesis and Neuroplasticity.

Physical exercise must be appropriate. This means it must be challenging and have novel aspects that stretch our physical limits. Research now shows that certain types of physical exercise get the job done better than others.

Recommended type and nature of Exercise

Effective physical exercise that stimulates the brain and Neuroplasticity should last thirty minutes each session and for five days, or times, a week. This exercise can be composed of various elements, notably, aerobic or cardio; strengthening using machines or free weights and balance using a balance board or ball.

This is the recommended mix:-

- Aerobic exercise—four times a week and at 60% of our maximum recommended age-related rate;
- Strength building—twice a week, using strength building machines or bands;
- Balance—twice a week for 30 minutes using an exercise ball or other tools.

This physical exercise affects all age groups. The aerobic or cardio exercises can consist of brisk walking, jogging, tennis, and the use of machines, such as treadmills, Stairmasters, rowing and elliptical machines.

Strength building needs to be progressive and incremental and once we have attained one level it helps to progress to the next. Personal Trainers can be very helpful in this regard.

Balance practice helps build confidence and helps overcome many issues that can challenge our brains and our belief in our abilities. Yoga can also be beneficial here.

The benefits to our well-being will take a few months; we need to maintain the schedule and life-style modification, and as Neuroplasticity is triggered and it will make the changes sustainable over time. The "use it or lose" tenet will play a role if the exercise is dropped without some form of maintenance.

Benefits from exercise

Benefits from Neuroplasticity triggered by physical exercise can include:-

- Increase in speed of processing information;
- Faster thinking;
- Improvement in memory recall;
- Probable slowing of "normal" aging;
- Increase in abilities to self-motivate and motivate others.

Moreover recent research by M.J. Friedrich (2008) indicates that physical exercise can extend the protection offered by the 'flu vaccine, and it helps our immune system and accelerates bodily healing.

B.   Mental and Intellectual activities

Another effective way to stimulate our brains in order to provoke Neuroplasticity is by mental or intellectual exercise. These exercises help us maintain our mental acuity, and refine our mental flexibility, agility and adaptability, and circumvent gradual decline over time. As with physical exercise, some mental exercises are more appropriate than others.

The essential components involve putting our brain cells to effective use by ensuring that our intellectual activities are challenged by something difficult and yet within our reach; it also helps stimulate the brain when the mental exercise is new or has new components that add to the challenge. This provokes the creation of new brain cells and increases the rate of survival of existing ones; moreover the process strengthens the pathways in existing neural networks and builds new connections.

As with physical exercise, the challenges presented by mental exercise increase the secretion of the Brain-Derived Neurotrophic Factor, BDNF, which helps neurons grow and stay healthy. This is evidenced by the fact that London cab drivers, who have to learn, and are tested on, complex routes throughout London, have a larger hippocampus section of the brain and higher levels of BDNF than do bus drivers in London who just follow a set bus route pattern.

Boosting our intellectual activities can take many forms, such as, Bridge, Sudoku, Crossword puzzles, learning a new language, learning to play the piano or learning a new piano score, or learning another language. The mental exercise must be challenging and novel and requires us to pay attention.

Increasing our mental agility allows us to achieve more balance in our lives by increasing our ability to focus, and shifting the focus of our emotions away from issues that cause stress or are unsettling. Furthermore boosting our mental sharpness helps ensure a better quality of life; after-all it is much less desirable to live longer if we cannot recall simple information or find that we are no longer able to perform simple mental tasks.

As with physical exercise, mental exercise is practiced, or used, at least five hours a week—generally over most days of the week. After about two months changes will occur and we are able to solidify our changed boost in intellectual awareness, accuracy and speed of processing in our brain's structure by using Neuroplasticity.

Challenge of Middle Age

It is as we get into our middle age and onwards, that perversely we run the greatest danger of inadequately challenging our mental faculties. This is because we have already acquired multiple skills, and have made many life decisions and have acquired significant life experiences. Hence, there is more of a temptation to stick with patterns or activities we prefer or know, and cruise along in comfort while perhaps our minds wander to other matters. Doing mental or intellectual activities with this mindset is like being on automatic pilot and does nothing to stimulate our brains, or will it provoke Neuroplasticity.

So even if an activity looks as though it could be handled easily without undue attention and effort, we need to build-in more challenge so that there are new aspects to consider or learn and the activity makes us face up to problems or issues we need to resolve. Wisdom often does come with age but Brain Fitness only grows by our interest in continual mental sharpness to tackle new and exacting strategies, which may include bridge or in artwork. These require our full attention and intense focus and concentration.

Benefits from Intellectual exercise

— Faster thinking

By using any or all of the three stimulants that boost Brain Fitness, but especially mental acuity ones, we will, according to Michael Merzenich, who wrote the text and features in the PBS video "The Brain Fitness Program," be able to train our brains to speed up so that they fire more quickly, and data is processed faster with less down time between firings.

Using this do-it-yourself Brain Fitness Program, we can to improve the accuracy of our perceptions, their precision, our thinking speed and our memory and we can do this at any age or stage of our lives.

— Paying Attention

A major part of improving our mental awareness is connected to mindfullness, which involves being attentive and heedful of our social and external environments. By paying attention and keeping a sharper focus we are able to discern the challenges and novelty involved in our behavior, and stimulate our brains to generate Neuroplastic activities.

This enables us to create new synapses or connections between neurons and strengthen the whole linkage apparatus. In response to stimuli, both internal and/or external, our brains can undergo re-organization and re-structuring throughout our lives, but this change can only happen when triggered by one of the three stimulants and most significantly when we pay attention. Even if the other activities are present there is no change without attention.

Work by Rueda, Posner, Rothbart in 2005, divides attention into three separate aspects.

These are:-

- Keeping alert;
- Orienting or focus;
- Ability to regulate emotions.

When we maintain a watchful and alert state, we are then more likely to notice activities going on around us or even within us. Thus, we can orientate, or focus, our senses on the information that we want or need. This allows us to regulate our emotional responses and manage our attention, so that it is focused on the attainment of our chosen goals for planning purposes.

Paying attention is crucial for any change, and is the key to all decision-making. It is also vital for an effective use of our memory; if we fail to pay attention then we are unlikely to input clear messages into our brains, which always results in unclear responses.

The good news is that we can learn to pay attention. Moreover, once we have it and use it, we are able to trigger Neuroplasticity and hopefully positive change.

— Memory

To pass any test during our formative years, we are told we need to memorize things. This essentially means we learn to rote-memorize so that we can repeat the data parrot fashion. While this may have some appeal and may get us through tests we generally can only retain data for a day or two, which simply does nothing to boost our memory powers.

Boosting our memory requires reflection of the core components of long-term memory. These components include the ways we encode a message and get the information into our brains; secondly the ways we retain the data and how we keep it stored in our brains; and finally the ways we recall or retrieve the data and put it to use.

Memory works by the nerve cells firing a transmitter signal between each other. Consequently, when we learn a new word in French, for instance, our nerve cells busily fire off a neurotransmitter signal between each other. If this occurrence is rarely repeated and we hardly use that word again, if ever, then the attraction between the synapses diminish and we cannot recall the word.

If on the other hand we do use the word frequently, then there is repeated activation and the synapses grow, and more Brain-Derived Neurotrophic Factor, BDNF, is produced, which permits more sprouting of new synapses; this reinforces the whole positive cycle and improves the functioning of neurons, improves and strengthens the pathways and increases the counterbalance to cell deaths.

In other words having a good memory is more than just having a lot of data filed away but also the ability to access it and use it appropriately. There are three parts to memory, which are:-

- Inputting Data,
- Recollection of the Data,
- Retrieving—for personal use.

The clearer we can input the data, the more likely we will be able to find the data and retrieve it for our later use. Often if our hearing is distorted then the data we input can be tainted. Messages that are inputted clearly are easier to recollect. However, if the data is inputted in a blurred way, then we often have more difficulty in recollecting the stored data. Some ways we can remember more easily is by:-

- Re-experiencing the emotion that can enhance recollection;
- Paying attention to a specific element;
- Aids can include mnemonics or grouping into categories.

Retrieval is the third element. This is essential for functional memory because mere recollection of facts does not help us draw on those facts to help make future decisions.

Both the encoding and retrieval processes are always selective as we cannot encode or decode all the details. Due to this selective process there will be variations. Moreover, we tend to select items that fit with who we are now. This may explain why we may remember something vividly yet it is at variance with the memory of the "same" past event recollected by a sibling or spouse. Hence, significantly our recollections may not always represent an absolute truth.

— Ability to forget

Ironically one of the most important facets of having a good memory is an ability to forget! This is dramatically illustrated in the 2008 book by Jill Price, in which she illustrates her inability to forget. The book describes her phenomenal ability to recollect data and dates throughout her life from early childhood. Yet she is unable to forget, which means she has retained all her childhood fears and anxieties. The book depicts a relatively recent incident that happened to her, then in early middle age, when she is confronted by a dog and re-experiences her fear of dogs generated when she was a child. Without an ability to forget, Ms. Price remembers every negative event that has ever happened in her life, which can dramatically stymie all forward movement in her life.

This is a daunting prospect, and we take for granted that we generally do have an ability to forget, or maybe to alter that recollection to make it fit with who we are now. This allows us to progress with our lives and enable us to override some emotions; in this way we can overcome some negativities of our past and we are able to build success out of the lessons learned from failures.

— Tips on Boosting our Memory

Memory begins with encoding any message before it can be stored and later retrieved, and to do this effectively requires active or careful listening to ensure that an accurate and clear message is received and can be properly encoded for storage. If it is not clear then chances are greater that the message retrieved will not be clear either. We can boost our ability to recollect a clear message if we listen attentively in the first place. As the old adage goes "muddied" meaning in means "muddied" meaning out.

Using good listening skills also permits us to distinguish between the foreground message input and any background noise, such as loud music playing. This takes some practice and the younger generation seems to be able to distinguish between competing sounds more easily, and often do their homework while watching TV. For people who find this more of a challenge, we can, with a little practice, learn to shift our focus to the sound of the message. When this happens we are able to hear more accurately, and can encode more exactly; all of which speeds up our processing speed and improves our retention and retrieval as demonstrated by better performance in memory and attention tests.

C. Socialization

"Few people are capable of expressing with equanimity opinions which differ from the prejudices of their social environment. Most people are even incapable of forming such opinions."—Albert Einstein.

We tend to seek out our social environments that best mirror our own views, and when that happens, the fit feels comfortable. However, we all have many groups in which we socialize. These can include our families, whether extended or otherwise, and groups that relate to what we do and believe; these can include school meetings, church events, choirs, community associations, bridge groups and our various types of sports groups.

Whether the fit is perfect or not, these are opportunities to socialize in ways that often challenge us mentally or intellectually, physically, or give us opportunities to parade our social skills.

The purpose of the group will alter our perception of what is expected of each member. The most important aspect of social engagement is we are obliged to meet with a range of people and exercise our own social and relationship skills. This requires a set of activities that may be generally less effective on brain growth than mental or physical activities, but, nonetheless can help in the neurogenesis process; especially if the socialization presents mental or physical stimulation over a specific period of time.

Being with other people can change the focus of our thinking and feeling and may contribute to some stress reduction, or change of focus that provides new challenges; all of which can stimulate our brains towards more BDNF production and Neuroplastic changes.

Stimulants and reduction of future risks

These three activities, whether physical, mental or social are effective stimulants, and all are capable of nudging the brain into Neuroplastic activity with the consequent extra production of BDNF; moreover, there is some evidence that the more we do so, the more we build up insurance against future problems.

Evidence by M. Mitka in 2001 shows that mental and physical activity and socialization are key factors in reducing the risk of mental impairment later as we age. Indeed Mitka recommends that instead of telling people "to take it easy" it is preferable to encourage physical and mental activities as means to maintain and develop our brain-power. For mental activities, Mitka especially recommends that we explore challenging activities such as:-

- Tricky mental posers, exploring new ways to paint or draw, exploring different strategies in bridge or chess;
- Learn a new language or develop existing foreign language skills;
- Use of Meditation, deep relaxation, yoga or tai chi.

Summary

- The concept of Brain Fitness includes:-
  - o Mastery over cognitive abilities;
  - o Use of Neurogenesis and Neuroplasticity;
  - o Benefits—faster thinking, memory and better recall.
- Neurogenesis is the growth of new neurons and strengthening of connections.
- Neuroplasticity directs our brains to be malleable and alter their functions and structures in our brain circuitry due to the increase in BDNF.
- Activities that stimulate Neuroplasticity are;
  - o Physical Exercise;
    - The most effective one;
  - o Mental Exercise;
    - Helps faster thinking, attention and memory.
  - o Socialization;
    - Can practice social skills and mental acuity.
- All effective stimulating activities must require:-
  - o Focus, Challenge and Novelty.
- Brain Quiz.

Brain Quiz No. 1:

Tipping the Scales

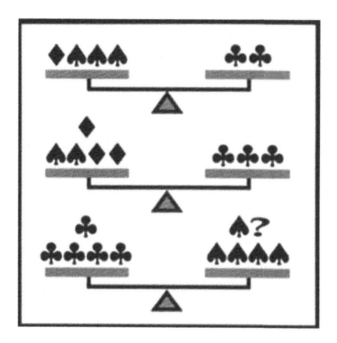

The top two scales are in perfect balance.
How many diamonds will be needed to balance the bottom set?

Solution is at the end of the book.
[Based on Quiz at *www.SharpBrains.com*].

Chapter Two

About Neuroplasticity

"The second half of a man's life is made up of nothing but the habits he has acquired during the first half."—Fyodor Dostoevsky

We now know that Dostoevsky's above quote no longer fits with our appreciation that our brains can grow new cells and adapt new functions and structures using Neurogenesis and Neuroplasticity. These days we can simply repeat the patterns we have acquired earlier in our lives as Dostoevsky suggests, or we can choose to change them.

Redesigning the Brain and Neuroplasticity

Neuroplasticity can work in two directions; it is responsible for deleting old connections as frequently as it enables the creation of new ones. Through this process, called "synaptic pruning," connections that are inefficient or infrequently used are allowed to fade away, while neurons that are highly valued and replete with information will be preserved, strengthened, and the synapses grow to be denser.

Closely tied in with the pruning process, then, is our ability to learn and to remember. While each neuron acts independently, learning new skills may require large collections of neurons to be active simultaneously in order to process neural information; thus the more neurons that are activated, the better we will learn.

The clear implication of this new knowledge about the Neuroplastic revolution is the way in which our emotions, such as, love or grief, or our thought patterns like addictions can change our brains. The architecture of our brains varies from person to person depending on our profile; this we now know can change over the course of our lives depending on our choices. One such action might be to speed up change to our brain's architecture by certain stimulants, such as physical activity or intellectual pursuits that ratchet up the production of BDNF and Neuroplasticity and also create new neurons using Neurogenesis.

Positive Neuroplasticity

Neuroplasticity has the effect of reinforcing an old or new patterns in the brain. When we think of change we generally think that it will be for the better; it often is but that is not always the case. Change can go both ways and in some circumstances we can reinforce, or set a pattern that is not the way we necessarily want to go.

A simple way to imagine the effect of Neuroplasticity is to consider a skier forging a new path down a slope covered with deep fresh snow. The first few times down the skier forges a pathway and it is quite hard work; then once the outline is traced down the slope the skier chooses that same pathway and gets into a groove. Neuroplasticity works the same way. Over a number of repetitions we become grooved into a new pattern. That pattern, or in terms of the skier the track, may or may not be favorable but our brains accept this modification as the way to go. The choice is ours.

Brain Fitness looks at ways to adjust our lifestyle by using Breakthrough Training to align our actions with our preferred outcomes, and then using the Neuroplasticity in a positive way to reinforce that new way of life by solidifying it as our new "usual" way of behaving. A typical 30 year old person, for instance, has a vocabulary of about 30,000 words, and often the extent of the vocabulary declines as the person ages. Statistically a mature adult has a 50:50 chance of ending life "non-compus mentus". Yet with Brain Fitness and positive Neuroplasticity, we can change those odds dramatically, and strengthen our brains and even regain some of the lost ground.

A further illustration of positive Neuroplasticity is where one hemisphere of the brain is damaged, and the intact hemisphere may take over some of the other's functions. The brain compensates for damage by reorganizing and forming new connections between intact neurons. It is Neuroplasticity that allows us to compensate for irreparably damaged or dysfunctional neural pathways by strengthening or rerouting our remaining ones. For this to happen and the reconnections to take place, the neurons need to be stimulated by a number of interactions that may begin with specific types of activity.

Positive effects of Neuroplasticity can also help people who have suffered changes in their brains due to a stroke or having lost their sight. Through the actions of growing new neurons and strengthening certain pathways the brain can compensate functionally for some part of the damage; compensation may take the form of helping blind people, who rely on Braille, develop an expansion of the area in the brain that deals with processing inputs from the index finger that follows the Braille. The brain may do some re-wiring to better equip us to read Braille more effectively and accurately. In this way the brain is capable of allowing blind people to use their visual cortex for other functions that may permit better hearing or touch.

Our brains' need for re-confirmation can be positive as it allows for some experimentation when, for instance, we want to change our emotions and thinking; it provides opportunities for unlearning that is also crucial in Neuroplasticity. With an unlearning capability we can allow in new emotions, thoughts and behaviors. The grieving process can, in most cases, show how we may grieve in multiple and profound ways for some time, but, if we are fortunate, we may gradually are able to build other emotions that allow more self-reliance and wider composite self-image of our lives and capabilities.

Negative Neuroplasticity

Not all forms of Neuroplasticity adaptations are positive. If we are constantly grooved into doing something in a negative way then the brain can make that adaptation permanent. Consequently any re-organization by the brain that becomes solidified can have positive or negative impact on our lives. Once the changes are accepted as enduring by our malleable brains, reversing the modification is complicated and the alternative must be grooved into the brain like a skier forging another path through the deep snow.

As a consequence we can opt for changes that actually make our situation worse. This can happen with deaf people who may suffer from a continual ringing in their ears because their neurons had been starved for sound and Neuroplasticity provides the ringing sound.

Our Brains and Change

Do our brains change constantly? Yes and No. Our brains are capable of change all through our lives. Yet the re-structuring of our brains, through Neuroplasticity, only occurs if certain conditions are present. These are:-

- We have to repeat the path or mental track many times before the change sticks;
- Our brains only look for different routes when encouraged or forced to do so;
- Otherwise we have natural "roadblocks" that send our brain back to our customary ways.

This is one of the reasons why dieting or smoking cessation takes some time, because the change can be introduced but unless the more customary approach is blocked, it is easier to revert to the previous pattern. The repetition of the new pattern is essential and must endure for many weeks; moreover we must focus and pay attention to the new pattern to encourage our brains to truly change and adapt to our new environment and circumstances. Many of us have anecdotal stories about people who are unable to switch from some form of addiction or repeated behavioral pattern unless they focus intently on the new behavior and repeat it consistently over several weeks.

Paying Attention

The basis of all change is our focus and our ability to pay attention; indeed focus and being attentive are pre-conditions for change. Although we can learn new things at any age, we have to want that new knowledge by demonstrating our motivation and level of focus. A youth, for instance, who wants to spend a year in France may well face starvation or other more subtle types of deprivation if she cannot make herself understood in the native language; consequently her motivation to pay attention is a lot higher than for someone living in the USA with a full time occupation and who takes language classes once a week as a way of meeting people.

Our brains are totally capable and adaptable to learn throughout our lives, but that change will depend heavily on our motivation and the extent of our focus and ability to pay attention.

Normal Aging

Using modern technological devices we can observe what is happening in the brain, and this helps ascertain the picture of the normal aging process. We can track our brains development from our earliest years and adolescence through to our current age or older and observe the lessening of the tissue. If we are to be successful with Brain Fitness change, we need an image of the normal process and proceed from there.

Existing data indicates that normal aging will have an impact on various cognitive functions, such as, the precision of memory, hearing and the speed of data processing. Yet Neurogenesis can provide much compensation; it enables us to activate our brains, which we can do in positive ways by enhancing our learning capabilities using keen focus and attentiveness, and by boosting our emotional intelligence abilities that give us greater personal awareness and improve our relationship talents.

One of the changes due to normal aging that we can see using modern technologies is some deterioration in the quality of our synapses that may be due to some erosion of the myelin coating of these connections; this change can affect our balance, or sense of balance, and sometimes our hearing accuracy. Fortunately, we know that are brains are not hardwired and they can deploy Neuroplasticity to re-wire or re-structure themselves in order to provide alternate ways of behaving or, in some cases, this re-structuring can fix damaged areas of our brains so that a form of functionality is regained.

Normal aging—Cognitive decline

It shows up in the little things first. It becomes harder to remember people and places and we have more difficulty pulling on the data we have stored away in our brains for relevant situations. We all experience some of these difficulties, but generally we find ways to overcome them to help our retrieval of the memories we need. However, if left unimpeded without triggering the beneficial effects of Neuroplasticity, these difficulties can grow until we ultimately lose track of things that shaped our life and made us who we are.

Normal Aging—Memory

Memory is keenly associated with aging. There are multiple factors involved in having a good and accurate memory, which we may neglect over time. It is important that we listen actively without being distracted so that we are able to file away the memory. As we have more and more data stored in our memory banks over time, we do tend to be more selective in choosing what we remember to fit with the image of who we are now. This is a normal process and we are inclined to have clearer pictures of like-minded individuals or events.

A major reason for memory loss as we age is the trouble we have in encoding or registering new events because processing time slows down, and we experience declines in the accuracy, strength and sharpness of our perceptions. If we insert unclear memories into our memory bank then in all likelihood we will have an unclear recall or recollection.

Part of the reason for the lack of clarity may be due to an inability to hear speech accurately, and this makes it harder to recollect clearly and remember and use words. Noisy backgrounds can exacerbate the difficulty. If untreated this can lead to gradual neglect and our brains' malleable nature can contribute to the decline. Indeed, some people choose to withdraw from embarrassment that further reinforces the downward spiral.

We can choose positive Neuroplasticity so that our brains learn new ways to work effectively by boosting our focus and paying keen attention in order to regain more clarity.

Neuroplasticity and Traumas and Disorders

Neuroplasticity allows the neurons, or brain cells, to compensate for injury and disease. Due to the malleability of our brains, or Neuroplasticity, we are able to "repair" damaged or disabled parts of our brain, and thereby recuperate or improve functions that otherwise might have been lost due to trauma, disease, or genetic misfortune.

Trauma

Trauma can re-shape our brains so that they handle inputs differently, sometimes with a positive result, or sometimes with a more damaging result. The brain views most changes, whether negative or positive, as temporary at first, but when re-confirmed by repetition over time they are considered more permanent.

In the past, we used to consider that any trauma that occurred after adolescence would make adaptability to the new circumstances almost impossibly hard for the brain. Yet, we now know that Neuroplasticity can work throughout our lives, and Neuroplastic responses can assist some recoveries from head injuries, brain diseases, or cognitive disability. Trauma impacts the map of our brain and permits parts that "normally" would have certain functions take on replacement and different functions.

This can have a positive impact, as recent studies demonstrate that persons who lose their sight after the age of fourteen, and who had a visual cortex that used to receive signals from the eyes, can begin to receive messages into the visual cortex from other sources. The Brain circuitry can re-organize to permit cross-model re-assignment that allows the visual cortex to take on hearing or greater touching abilities.

Sometimes the impact can be more negative, as in the case of people with no hearing or have lost their hearing but crave sound, and courtesy of Neuroplasticity the brain may provide Tinnititis, or ringing in the ears, which can be a major irritant.

Disorders

This is an area that requires more research, as the data is indicative but not conclusive. Various studies, for instance, show possible links between low levels of BDNF in humans and disorders such as depression, obsessive compulsive disorder, Alzheimer's, Huntington's, Rett's Syndrome and consequently expedient action is advised.

Alzheimer's

First diagnosed in 1906, Alzheimer's frequently co-occurs with insomnia, depression, anxiety, agitation and aggression. Unfortunately by the time it is diagnosed accurately the damage to the brain is significant and as yet not shown to be reversible since neurons get worn down and synapses erode; people also lose their ability to adapt to excessive energy demands, anxiety and stress. In cases where synaptic decay outpaces the new construction, synaptic activity decreases and dendrites retract, and the blood supply to the brain diminishes. This leads to a communication dysfunction or loss of efficiency and can lead to cognitive decline—including Alzheimer's or other forms of degenerative disorders.

In their 2008 paper that outlines an Alzheimer Action Plan, Dr. Doraiswamy and other leading clinical researchers in this field, estimate that Alzheimer's affects over 5 million Americans and an even larger number have mild to moderate memory loss and run the risk of developing the disease.

We attach much value to the maintenance of our cognitive and emotional functions for our independence, productivity and quality of life. While reversal of Alzheimer's is hypothetical at this stage, what we do know is that starting with Brain Fitness programs as early as feasible, can impact this whole process by helping the person keep his brain better connected, more resilient and allow that person to stay active longer.

The idea is to stimulate Neuroplasticity, and while this will not automatically stop diminishing capacities, it can have an impact that acts as a sort of antidote to stave off further declines. This notion is reinforced by C.K. Cassel's 2002 study that argues in favor of using Neurogenesis and Neuroplasticity to stave off this progressive disease rather than we spend huge sums on alternative therapies that lack any scientific evidence to support their use.

Moreover, recent work conducted by Dr. Bennett at the Rush University Medical Center in Chicago indicates the possibility that we may be able to use Brain Fitness programs to build reserves that are able to resist decline for longer time periods; these reserves, it is suggested, can act like an insurance policy and protect people from developing the disease.

Addictions

Clear examples of long-term Neuroplastic changes in the brain are illustrated by addictions that may even start as short-term ways of coping. They may include drugs, alcohol, and tobacco, gambling or even running; these activities can become deeply ingrained as the brain adapts to this new way of being, and makes the Neuroplastic changes accordingly to incorporate them in what is "normal".

These plastic changes can cause long-lasting changes to the brain. One effect is the build-up of tolerance to the substance; this can lead to wanting more of the substance for the equivalent effect even if this action defies logic. This has also been demonstrated by the so-called ice-cream experiments that found levels of satisfaction diminish as more and more of the ice-cream is consumed, but the recollection of the intense pleasure from the first bite far outweighs the lessening effect of pleasure from the fourth or fifth bite of ice-cream.

Running is another addiction as it prompts the release dopamine in the brain, which gives us a surge of energy and prompts an experience of pleasure; this can be positive where it replaces other sources of dopamine, but can be less positive where it becomes an ingrained habit that we need in our lives.

Strokes

Neuroscientist, Michael Merzenich, who features prominently in the 2007 PBS Brain Fitness program, has spent considerable time exploring an avenue to help people with learning disabilities or strokes form new neural connections by getting neighboring healthy neurons to fire together and thereby wire together.

This also is the approach taken by Taub in his 2006 work on "constraint-induced therapy", which showed that even when a stroke has damaged a brain region, its previous function is not irretrievably lost. His work indicates that therapy-aided recovery can occur with stroke victims, and he was able to show that the brain is able to recruit nearby neurons to perform functions of damaged ones, and enable stroke patients who have lost the use of a limb to send signals to permit movement. Few conditions are as scary as strokes when part of our brain dies, but Taub was able to demonstrate that as long as there is adjacent living tissue and because that is plastic, it may take over.

Brain researcher, Dr. Jill Bolte Taylor, tells of her rare form of stroke in her 2006 book that shut down her left hemisphere of her brain. This is where language, logic and linear thought are based. For months she was not able to walk, talk or read, nor could she write about or recall events in her life. Remarkably this shut down had the effect of silencing her own mental dialogues and rantings and left her in a state of harmony. She was able to regain full brain function after eight years of rehabilitation, but is still able to access a state of complete peace and well-being at will.

Speculation surrounds why, after a long period of rehabilitation, she was able to recuperate most of her lost functions, and she also retained access to that harmonious state. It is possible that this was due to her focus and attention that she directed to the richness of the present moment and her awareness, and these factors helped her override preoccupations with projected fears, or concerns.

Making new connections

Much of the work with stroke patients is based on Hebb's rule in 1949, which made the connection with neighboring neurons. We now know that when two neurons fire at the same time repeatedly, or where one causes the other to fire, then chemical changes occur in both so that the two neurons have a bond. This is expressed succinctly by neuroscientist Carla Schatz who stated that "Neurons that fire together wire together" or things that happen together actually bond together.

Our brain thrives on making new connections—especially if it is being stimulated and constantly re-wiring and adapting. We can use what has become know as the Hebb rule to our advantage by combining activities so that the positive aspect of one will rub off onto the other. This can include the pleasure of listening to a particular book on Playaway, or CD, while working out on an elliptical machine, or having a delicious meal while socializing at an event. This brings associated pleasure and weakens or eases anxiety or stress.

Neuroplasticity—major factor in Brain Fitness

Neuroplasticity can make a difference to our lives by the enormous benefits we can derive from greater Brain Fitness. This also is true for cases of rehabilitation and injuries—previously thought irreparable; likewise in cases where we may have suffered a stroke, are dyslexic or are blind. Increasingly, evidence shows that Neuroplasticity, or malleability of our brains, assists learning and adaptation and our brains can produce new neurons and can re-structure our brain's circuitry. Major stimulants for Neuroplasticity include physical and mental exercise as well as socialization; these will require our focus and attention and they must present challenge and some novelty.

We can further help this process by gaining more mastery over our thoughts and feelings so that they trigger more beneficial chemicals in our brains that spur Neurogenesis, and Neuroplasticity.

Summary

- Neuroplasticity allows us to re-design the brain.
- Neuroplasticity can be positive;
  - Its advantages include new behaviors and recuperative possibilities.
- Neuroplasticity can also be negative.
- Our Brains and Change;
  - We can only change where we pay attention.
- Benefits of Neuroplasticity.
  - Memory, Faster Thinking, Attention and Focus.
- Normal process of aging.
  - Normal Memory loss;
  - Normal Cognitive decline.
- Traumas and Disorders and Addictions.
- Ways our Brains make new connections.
- Neuroplasticity is a major factor in Brain Fitness;
  - Stimulated by multiple factors-notably exercise.
- Brain Quiz

Brain Quiz No. 2:

Find third word associated with both these words

For instance, if the first pair is PIANO and LOCK—then the answer is KEY as there are KEYS on a piano and we use a KEY to lock doors.

- SHIP—CARD
- TREE—CAR
- SCHOOL—EYE
- PILLOW—COURT
- RIVER—MONEY
- BED—PAPER
- ARMY—WATER
- TENNIS—NOISE
- EGYPTIAN—MOTHER
- SMOKER—PLUMBER

Solutions are at the end of the Book.
[Based on Quiz at *www.SharpBrains.com*].

Part Two

Breakthrough Training
and Brain Fitness

Chapter Three

Breakthrough Training—Limits of Thinking

"What luck for rulers that men do not think"—Adolf Hitler

As we progress into twenty first century we are dealing with a new paradigm that has a new way of looking at what constitutes success and right thinking. In the past we wanted to approach perfection and think the right way. Now the focus of our new paradigm is on making things work, and where necessary, making adaptations to ensure they are functional and rational. This enables us to benefit from the various tools of Breakthrough Training that help us make effective changes to our behaviors.

One set of Breakthrough Training tools enable us to explore our cognitive capacities to think and assess their adequacy and where and how change may be appropriate.

Breakthrough Training and Thinking

Breakthrough Training incorporates cognitive and dialectical behavioral techniques that help modulate our ways of thinking and our thought patterns in ways that are effective and assist attain our goals. Logic plays a big role in our ability to think and the underlying rational. Sometimes we may consider that our thoughts are circular, and even at times that we can switch off our thinking by not fully processing the implications of a thought; both repetition of thoughts and our ability to switch off are possible and even likely at times. Yet, we can modulate and evaluate our thoughts so that they best suit our needs.

Our thoughts are not set in stone, but are changeable—especially when we systematically apply Breakthrough Training's behavioral tools that enable us to plumb down into our logic and the influence our past experiences and feelings have on the ways we think.

Thinking and Neuroplasticity

This approach takes a more open position that allows us to envisage options about the limits of thinking. Yet, how does this fit with developments in Neuroscience, and our awareness of our ability to grow new neurons and make them malleable? In effect our thoughts and feelings are closely tied to activities of our brains. Both thoughts and feelings trigger the production of Norepinephrine and Dopamine that then trigger changes in the production of Brain Derived Neurotrophic Factor or BDNF, which is essential to spur Neuroplasticity.

All changes to our thinking will set off two sets of actions. First, we can change our patterns of thinking that may allow us to better direct our thoughts using behavioral techniques; this will take account of our focus and environment. Our new patterns of thinking will modify the levels of chemicals released in the brain and will have an indirect impact on Neuroplasticity. Secondly, Neuroplasticity itself can be stimulated by the right stimuli, such as physical exercise, which is rewarding, riveting and novel. The effect can solidify changes to our thinking, providing they are sufficiently reinforced. Thereafter the Neuroplasticity can also reinforce our thought patterns. Hence the two are inextricably linked.

Of course we can induce chemical changes by taking legal or illegal drugs and these can have temporary effects or may become more enduring addictions.

Feelings and Thoughts

We often we describe our thinking and our feelings interchangeably. Sometimes when we ask someone about what they think is happening that person will give a response that describes their feeling rather than their thoughts. We hear, for instance, comments such as "I feel you are driving too slowly" which actually is a thought, and a corresponding the feeling might be "I feel *irritated* that you are driving too slowly".

Thoughts and feelings are highly inter-related and yet are formed in different parts of our brain; moreover they are stored differently and every feeling we have ever experienced is stored in our long-term memory.

We can all do . . . Thinking

Yes—we all can think. Sometimes the same thought keeps percolating in our heads. Indeed Deepak Chopra (2008) once said we have 60,000 thoughts a day, and 95% of those thoughts are the same as we had yesterday! We have options to save this energy. We can circumvent circular thinking using the following tools and techniques that will help us identify our thoughts more precisely. These, then can be reinforced and solidified using our Neuroplastic capabilities.

I.   What are we thinking?

Sometimes we just don't know where to start in our consideration of what we are thinking about, and there are three simple tools that help us in this process.

   a.   The first to *observe* what is going on and experience what is happening without trying to alter or terminate it;
      i.   We often do well to take a step back for a better perspective;
      ii.   We observe the event without doing it;

   b.   The second step is to *describe* that event;
      i.   We apply verbal labels to the event or behavior;
      ii.   We can use videos or visualize the event we describe;

   c.   The third step is to *participate* in the event without seeking to impress or influence;

    i.   We must pay attention, even if this seems mechanical;

    ii. We can deflect our distracting thoughts by speaking and listening intently.

II. How are we thinking?

In reviewing our capacity to think, we can usefully consider how we are framing that thinking.

There are three ways we can ideally frame just how we are going about the thinking:-

  a) First—is to take a non-judgmental approach;

    i.   Events are neither good nor bad, but we do notice the consequences of each event;

    ii. Maintain impartiality and this helps observation

without attachment and we notice consequences
without ethics;

b) Secondly-is to focus on one thing at a time, with narrowed attention;
    i. This means managing distractions, both external and internal;
    ii. We must keep our focus on the present moment;

c) Third—is to adapt our way of thinking to what works and is effective;
    i. This requires us to measure against a clear priority or goal;
    ii. Also we need clear objectives or tactics to get there.

These simple techniques help us identify what we are thinking and how we are framing those thoughts. With practice these simple tools helps us focus on our priorities, and concentrate on goals. If we see the factors of "what" we are thinking or "how" we are thinking deviate from what we want to achieve, we can bring in changes that will meet our requirements. This can involve using rational thinking in our thought processes and by identifying areas where it is lacking.

Over time and with practice we gain more control over our processes of thinking, their content and we gradually are able to better direct our thoughts. We can also learn to shift our thinking into more positive and optimistic ways. To do so, we can run through the above questions and ask ourselves how a positive optimistic person would respond and practice those ways of thinking and behaving. This will helps us become more self-confident and trusting. As we repeat the kind of responses we desire, these patterns will fasten in our brains, through Neuroplasticity, and become our usual patterns of thinking.

Prosperity vs. Poverty Thinking

In these current times of economic disturbance, James Gottfurcht, Wealth Consultant and Clinical Psychologist, has concerns that many people have thought patterns that make them even more vulnerable to the economic turbulence. Gottfurcht's website and private consultations are geared to help people take charge and protect themselves by re-adjusting their thought patterns through a thorough examination of their life priorities and values. In particular, he addresses the issue of how we think and differentiates between Prosperity Thinking and Poverty Thinking.

His approach is to help his clients gain a better appreciation of their propensities towards these two different ways of thinking. The Prosperity Thinking approach generally implies a trusting attitude that things will work out, and is accompanied by personal confidence and self-esteem. While Poverty Thinking approach is a less trustful state and is more pessimistic with the view that things will not work out; often people with this type of thinking have lower self-esteem and confidence. These approaches can distort perceptions.

Distorted Thinking

Dr. Gottfurcht recommends that we focus on aspects that we can control; this excludes the overall negativity of financial events which are cyclical over the long run.

These are valuable ways to review a situation, and we can ask ourselves about our tolerance for risk, what our needs reality check-list includes, whether we have access to a support group and whether we use exercise for our well-being. In this way, we can review ways to take a more positive approach to situations over which we have little control and take action to re-assert reality into our thinking, where appropriate.

Using Neuroplasticity to enhance Thinking

Neurogenesis and Neuroplasticity create new neurons and strengthen their connections; this enables us to adopt new functions or structures and often solidifies patterns that have been repeated to make them more permanent. New ways of thinking can be reinforced so that they become entrenched and constitute our pattern of thinking.

As we develop our abilities to deploy Brain Fitness, our mental acuity, and other intellectual faculties can benefit greatly from the brain stimulating activities, such as, physical and mental exercise that promote Neuroplasticity, and that in turn can help us adapt our thinking capacities.

Novelty, Challenge and Focus

If there is no novelty, then we tend to operate in our comfort zones, and act and react in ways we know so well; it is as if we are working on autopilot which may save us energy, but generally is not very interesting, nor does it stimulate the Neuroplasticity of our brains.

Challenges can come in many forms. To best use physical and mental activities we need to move out of our comfort zones and put in incremental effort that may stretch our abilities, and yet achieve our new goal. Getting outside help through a trainer often helps us build-in additional challenges and novel approaches.

We also need to ensure that we pay attention, a point underscored by Dr. Michael Merzenich in the 2007 PBS video, who firmly states that we can only change things if we pay attention to them. This involves careful listening, a selective approach and focus rather than allowing distractions to deflect us from our goals.

Link between Thoughts, Feelings and Actions

There is a strong interplay between our thoughts, our feelings, and our actions. In fact, Behavioral science has established a simplified model that illustrates in a continually looping chain the close link between thoughts, feelings and actions or behaviors.

Behavioral Chain

The following chart is a simplified model of how we function in all our daily activities and it indicates how thoughts and emotions or feelings induce thoughts that lead to behaviors with consequences, which then trigger new feelings that in turn prompt thoughts and set off another action with consequences and the whole cycle begins again.

Table 1: Behavioral Chain

Feeling-Thought-Action Chain

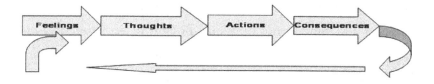

Table 1: Behavioral Chain. Based on work by Linehan, M. M. (1993) and Carr, J. E., & LeBlanc, L. A. (2003), adapted and modified by Ann J. Polya, Ph.D. (2009).

This behavioral chain depicts the strong link between feelings and our thoughts. An emotion or feeling will set off a thought and lead to some subsequent action. For instance, if we are feeling angry with Don, then we are more likely to think he is trying to manipulate us and our actions will be based on that thought.

If we wish to change the outcome, or our behavior, then we must modify our thinking or preceding feeling; one way to do this is to run through a whole scene writing out each step of the behavioral chain with a clear indication of our feelings, thoughts, and what we did and its consequences. We then can review our notes and indicate with a colored pen where we could have changed the outcome. In the vast majority of cases our best approach to change how we act by changing our thinking.

Our Thinking "Machines"

If we could imagine our brains were like computers that are dependent on rational data inputs, then we would have a rational way to make decisions. However, our brains are infinitely more complex and contain not only our thought patterns but also our emotions that include our memories. The following story indicates how two people can make decisions about the same incident for different reasons based on their priorities.

Consider the following story:-

Fred wants to purchase a house. His plan is to base his decision on logic and rationality. His wife Jean has a more emotive approach. He asks an expert to examine two houses of the same size. The expert's report finds 10 things to be corrected in each house, the estimated cost to fix House A is 5% less than House B, the real estate taxes are identical, as too are square footage, layout and external colors. House A purchase cost is 10% higher than House B, but House A has a small pool in the garden and has been repainted inside by a specialist, while House B has new heating and cooling system and is located in a quieter neighborhood.

Fred chooses House A, based on the available data. His partner Jean prefers the neighborhood of House B due to a previous bad experience with a neighborhood like that of House A; also she feels better to choose her own colors and design for House B. So her decision is in favor of House B.

Which way would you go?

There is no absolute answer. Yet this dilemma confronts us constantly. We all have a Fred side to us that takes a rational approach to decision making, and we generally have our Jean persona that is more taken with the emotional elements. Our brains confront this classic dilemma all the time.

The best way to resolve it is to consider our precise goals.

Goals

We need to ascertain our prime goals or targets and what we want to achieve. Vague and broad goals that could incorporate many things simply do not help. We need to define for ourselves exactly what we want. This can be our life's goals or our goal for what we want to achieve in this particular meeting. We do ourselves a big favor if we can ascertain, ahead of any decision, are our S-M-A-R-T goals, which are:-

- Specific,
- Measurable,
- Achievable,
- Realistic,
- Time-phased.

Setting our goals can save us a lot of time and can help us in our process of building new or more effective thought patterns. We can ensure the goals meet our S-M-A-R-T criteria and use them to help us assess our thinking and whether it gets us to the outcome we desire so that we can move forward rationally.

Summary

- Our Brains allow us the capacity to think and experience emotions.
- As part of Breakthrough Training, we can use behavioral techniques to modify our thought patterns.
- This triggers release of certain chemicals that indirectly prompt Neuroplasticity, as our brains are influenced by our thoughts and our feelings.
- We can use behavioral techniques to check our thoughts and their rationale;
  o Using queries on "what" we are thinking;
  o Using queries on "how" we are thinking.
- Brain Fitness stimulants prompt BDNF production and Neuroplasticity;
  o Neuroplasticity can solidify changes to our new thinking patterns stick.
- We can actively change our thinking to be more positive and optimistic.
- We need to be clear about our goals if we are to successfully direct our thinking.
- Brain Quiz.

Brain Quiz No. 3:

Memory and Thinking Skills

- Name the one sport in which neither spectators nor participants know the score until the contest ends.
- What famous North American landmark is constantly moving backward?
- Only two vegetables can produce for several growing seasons-all others are annuals. What are they?
- What fruit has its seeds on the outside?
- Name the one vegetable or fruit that is never sold frozen, canned, processed, or cooked.
- Name 5 things that you can wear on your feet beginning with the letter "S."

Solutions are at the end of the Book.
[Based on Quiz at *www.SharpBrains.com*].

Chapter Four

Breakthrough Training—Managing Emotions

"What others think of us would be of little moment did it not, when known, so deeply tinge what we think of ourselves."—Paul Valery

Breakthrough Training and Emotions

In this information age, we are exposed to reams and reams of data, and we need to store that data, and retrieve it when required. The inescapable aspect of all this data is that, even though classic economics pretends otherwise, emotions and feelings creep into many of the important decisions we make. Breakthrough Training includes a set of tools, derived from dialectal and cognitive behavioral dynamics that address managing our emotions by boosting our understanding of the feelings and forge strategies to alter our emotional reactions, where appropriate.

Our emotions are complex responses to life events that often reflect our experiences, values and morals. This is factored into the approach taken by Breakthrough Training, which facilitates ways to manage emotions and assess and ensure they are better serving our needs. Unlike dealing with thoughts this has little to do with logic.

Our brains are the repository for all emotions we have ever felt in our lives, whether they are conscious or sub-conscious. We can access them in several ways using Breakthrough Training behavioral tools that help us learn more about the nature of the emotions, how they are triggered and how certain strategies reduce their hold over us and put us back in the driver's seat to have our emotions work better for us.

Moreover, like our thought patterns, the more we are able to repeat these feelings, the more our brain's plasticity and malleability is able to make the changes stick.

Impact of Emotions

Our brains are constantly assessing what events mean; both in general and specific terms. We hold those meanings up against the yardstick of our goals. Emotions are a way of informing us whether that event is good or bad, and they stimulate us into appropriate action. They can be very useful guides for what we like or dislike, or whom we trust or mistrust.

Yet, it is rarely advisable to make important decisions about our future when we are experiencing strong emotions, whether it is fear, anxiety, panic or love. Applying logic will not help as rarely do emotional decisions comply with a rational approach. Instead we can deal with any problem-solving or decisions better if we start with a fuller picture of our emotional response; what is it telling us and why? Then we can address our options to bring ourselves back into balance so that we are in a better position to assess what we want.

Irrational, emotional decision-making is the basis of our current economic recession. What started as a situation where people, fueled by the herd factor that if X is making money then you should be too, even if you cannot rationally afford it, so you get a loan like many others. Then markets became alarmed as conditions began to look grim and panic spreads across the globe.

This economic downturn is partly driven by facts and partly driven by emotions according to the Dr Paul J. Zak, Director of the Center for NeuroEconomics at Claremont Graduate University. In a 2009 article, Dr. Zak illustrated his view that in times of economic uncertainty and recession, we become more fearful and stressed and our brains move into a survival mode; we are then more prone to be risk adverse as levels of the pleasure chemical Dopamine drop. In this highly emotionally charged environment, stress, fear and anger actually impede our brains from functioning well and we may hinder ways that boost our Brain Fitness.

Chemical reactions triggered by emotions

Each typical neuron, or brain cell, has over 100,000 connections but they are not all active at the same time. The pre-frontal cortex region of the brain is most affected by emotions, and it slows when we are bored or tired. It produces more dopamine and norepinephrine when under stress and this combined with the slow down sometimes produces a feeling that we are not in control. There may be times when we freeze or our mind goes blank, or we may react impulsively.

Research indicates that estrogen can provoke women to experience stress more readily than men; many men seem to experience greater difficulty with self-motivation. Consequently it is helpful to identify the gender and type of person and source of the emotion to that we are better placed to be of effective help. Helpful levers can include specific training, physical exercise, meditation, balanced nutrition, or some talk treatment, and possibly some form of social engagement.

Crossover effect of Emotions

It would seem that we need only to examine each emotion and its nature, and its triggers in order to understand what is happening. However, it is more complex as emotions have a crossover effects and our reactions can be influenced by other emotions, which may run counter to the advice being given. This has been illustrated by the recent work of Wharton Professor, Maurice Schweitzer and Francesca Gino of Carnegie Mellon University, who determined that emotions can be triggered by something in the past that is ostensibly irrelevant to the current situation. They found that clients who were angry with a spouse or co-worker were less likely to be receptive to the advice being given about a different matter.

We know that a person's mood can affect their whole way of thinking. A person, for instance, who is grieving the loss of a loved one is likely to go through the stages of grief, which are:—denial, anger, bargaining, depression and acceptance; while these stages are not ironclad, they nonetheless indicate the types of emotions that can sweep over the grieving person. Hence a person in grief may also be experiencing another strong emotion that will influence their thoughts and actions, even though that emotion may not have been immediately obvious.

Powerful Emotions

— Stress

This emotion stems from our primordial times when, many thousands of years ago, our human ancestors developed a "fight or flight" emotive reaction for self preservation in order to avoid being eaten by predators. Modern day threats are different, and yet feel just as real.

We all deal with some stress in our daily lives that generally lasts for short time periods. Our brains and bodies can handle the extra cortisol we produce, which can be energizing and helpful, as, for example, the prompting of salivation when we smell good food odors. Our response is modulated by our past experiences and often a mildly stressful situation is challenging and spurs prompter action with a positive effect. Stress that is tolerable varies from one person to another, and often depends on our level of good emotional support systems or our range of coping mechanism according to each need. However, when stress becomes chronic and is not alleviated by our supports and lasts and lasts, then this can have negative physical and mental implications.

Chronic stress can have many origins, and frequently they appear to have complex causes and often seem out of our direct control. Ongoing concern about financial matters, major family disputes, legal concerns are just a few possible causes. When we are afflicted with chronic stress, our personal production of key chemicals goes off balance and can severely impact our motivation to exercise, look after ourselves rationally, and may compel us to withdraw from being with others and impose other detrimental effects on our brains that compromise our abilities for Neuroplasticity.

With chronic stress our actions may freeze or we may become aggressive. We tend to view things in the short term as if that is what is needed to survive. It can lead to headaches, feeling pains in different parts of our bodies, and we may feel frazzled and run down. The frozen state can inhibit our ability to reflect adequately. Research by Brigit Kuehn in 2006 indicates that the changed levels of dopamine and norepinephrine, reduces that of BDNF, or Brain-derived Neurotrophic Factor, which decreases options for Neurogenesis and Neuroplasticity and all their benefits.

Typical chronic stress reactions have major physical repercussions; they may cause increases in our heart rate and blood pressure, and may put us more at risk for developing diabetes. This chronic stress causes us to produce extra cortisol that over a prolonged period of time can slow down our metabolism, which can cause us to gain weight or sometimes lose weight.

Frequently, we experience more cravings for fatty, salty and sugary foods and often accompanying the stress are major variations in our blood sugar levels that lead to greater mood swings and fatigue.

We can get into a vicious cycle so that mood swings propel emotional eating, and we pay less attention to balance our nutrition, and we tend to drop physical exercise from our to-do list due to our hectic schedule. Moreover, sustained stress tends to increase our propensity to store fat in our abdominal area.

This is becoming more and more widespread in our society as our minds are racing from everything we have to do, but we get less exercise as we spend precious moments sitting in traffic, clocking hours at our desks, juggling several jobs and seeking relief in front of the TV in exhaustion at the end of the day.

The five strategies, listed later in this chapter, provide effective tools to cope with this strong emotion.

— Fear

This too is a powerful emotion, and is often linked, or combined, with stress. Today's turbulent economic situation is a fertile ground for more and more people to feel threatened and fearful as the global economic downturn forms a backdrop, which we cannot readily change. In the grips of this emotion, as with chronic stress, we often feel overwhelmed and unable to take decisions. Sometimes we may freeze in the face of our natural biological "fight or flight" response that is a fast reaction in the brain that often precedes being able to see the danger; this in our modern day may not come from marauding lions but "attacks" by a predatory boss.

As with chronic stress we may have a racing heart, rise in blood pressure, we may become aggressive, and we will focus on the near-term. The emotion of fear can be generated by numerous causes and our potential threats can be real or imagined ones.

Fear is an unpleasant feeling, and like all emotions we have ever experienced it is stored in our memory bank. We frequently, consciously or sub-consciously, dig back into our past and retrieve data about how we then reacted. This way of dealing with this emotion may have worked well as a child, but may no longer work for us now, or it may still work.

Typical "fear" words include apprehension, anxiety, distress, dread, fright, horror, panic, shock, overwhelmed, and worry. As we become more aware of what is happening, we can take a step back, observe and identify the emotion that we are experiencing and what may have evoked this emotion. Some provoking situations might include an unfamiliar place, or somewhere, or with someone associated with a past hurt.

We cannot necessarily change the situation but we can change our exposure to the situation and our reactions. It is possible that underlying this emotion is a belief that we may be rejected or unsupported, and we may experience a knee-jerk reaction to re-assert control. The five coping strategies detailed later in this chapter are a fruitful approach to deal with with this emotion.

— Anxiety

Anxiety is a natural reaction to a threat and has similar elements to both the fear and stress reactions. Some level of anxiety can keep us alert and sharpen our attention. It may include a fear component in the way we might feel a lurch in our stomachs when a plane suddenly loses height due to turbulence. However, if we worry when there is no real threat, we move from worry into more chronic anxiety events; these can replicate themselves and spread so that more events cause us to feel strong levels of anxiety, and if left untended they can lead to panic attacks.

There is also a small contingent of people whose worries take on an extra dimension as they suffer from Obsessive Compulsive Disorder (OCD), and are scared of some impending harm, which they seek to avert through obsessive behaviors. These people are well advised to seek professional help for this disorder.

For most other people, it may often be helpful to discuss the feelings with someone else as the anxiety may stem from some misinterpretation or misunderstanding. Other sources of help include getting some exercise to give the thinking brain a "holiday", meditation and the five coping strategies detailed later.

— Love

Love can be a powerful emotion, and while we generally think of it positively, as it too can alter the chemical levels in our brain that can radically change how we act and react. According to Michael Craig Miller, M.D., in his 2008 Newsweek article, there is scientific evidence that love turns down, or even turns off, the reasoning part of our brain and also suspends our brain's judgment and fear centers. With this emotion, we may feel out of control and not appear to be operating rationally. This emotion of love truly may blind us to the power of logic and indeed limit our powers to differentiate between us.

Typically the emotion of love is linked with its related words, such as, adoration, affection, attraction, caring, sympathy, desire, charmed, kindness, and tenderness. We might experience this emotion when someone gives us a special present, or when sharing a special experience with another, or when we hear a particular piece of music that has meaning to us.

If this is something we want to address, the five strategies later in this chapter may help.

— Anger

Typically when we feel anger we are experiencing related feelings that can include aggravation, disgust, agitation, contempt, hate, hostility, or scorn. Frequently this emotion is accompanied by aggression or aggressive thoughts.

Anger can be set off by events, such as, loss of power or status, the theft of something we value, receiving insults or not having our expectations met.

This emotion often brings pain to us, and sometimes to others depending on how we react, and frequently we have a sense that we have not been treated fairly and that others do not understand because we are right and our way is the way. The five coping strategies assist coming to terms with this emotion.

Motivation's underlying Emotion

What motivates us is nearly always an underlying emotion that acts as a stimulus. If we feel we need to belong to a certain group or we need praise and encouragement because that was lacking in our childhood then those factors will rank highly amongst those that motivate us.

For most people major motivating influences are ways we can improve our living or working conditions, material benefits that can include salaries, inheritance or other core benefits, a heightened sense of belonging that might include membership of elite group, praise and encouragement and job security. These are ways to provide evidence of the type of emotion that will mobilize us into action or reaction.

Meditation and Stress study

In a joint study in 2007 between researchers at Dalian University of Technology in Dalian, China, and the University of Oregon, evidence was gathered on whether, or not, meditation could improve a person's attention and stress response.

The study was done in China and it randomly assigned forty college undergraduates to both control and experimental groups. One group received five days of meditation training, while the other got five days of relaxation training. Both groups were tested ahead of the study for their levels of attention and reaction to mental stress and after the study.

It was found that the group that received the meditation training showed greater improvement in their attention as measured by their ability to resolve conflict. Stress was induced by mental arithmetic. Both groups initially showed elevated release of the stress hormone cortisol following the math task, but after training the group with the meditation showed significantly more improvement in stress regulation and lower levels of anxiety, depression, anger and fatigue.

Meditation

Meditation is a proven means of stress reduction that enables mental training by allowing the mind to observe itself. It helps us focus on our thoughts, emotions and self-awareness and boosts our ability to pay attention to a single thing. We can develop better mental concentration and deep relaxation and it increases our ability to relax-as measured by our metabolic rate; it also can decrease anxiety and depression and can lower our cholesterol and blood pressure levels. It induces a state of restful alertness that allows us to quieten our minds so we have greater body-mind awareness, focus and clarity that allows introspection to re-visit and re-assess our emotions-whether positive or negative.

We can achieve more control over our thoughts and feelings in the process, and we can boost our positive approaches with greater recourse to compassion, empathy and fuller attention; moreover it can free our brains of negative tendencies that may include hatred or jealousy. As we gain focus, we increase our ability to resist distractions and bring things into sharper detail.

Meditation may involve some guidance, by a coach or recorded voice, or we can use our own guidance. There are many forms of meditation but they generally deploy breathing techniques, the use mental imagery and soothing music in the background to heighten the relaxed state. We can meditate in groups or alone. We need sufficient time, and a quiet place to sit still and be silent.

The art of meditation is the art of listening with our total being. When we listen to the words and allow ourselves to picture the images, we get a sharper awareness that we can bring into our daily lives. We learn to experience silence with no effort and we learn how to be unaffected by distractions.

At first we may notice extraneous noises and other distractions, which are often the effects of accumulated stress. Gradually we gain more confidence and learn to let go of tensions so that we can enjoy the meditative process and use this opportunity to learn. The expansion of our awareness brings a clearer picture of our thoughts and emotions. We learn to operate in the present, and with practice the whole meditative process gets easier so that our enhanced attention and focus better equip us to handle today's mass of free floating information.

Meditation, with its focused breathing and consequent heightened state of awareness, can assist us re-assess our thoughts and feelings and reduce levels of tension, fear, anger, and stress in our lives.

Visualization

As Michael Merzenich, said in the 2007 PBS documentary, our brains are massively remodeled by our exposure to the Internet, television, movies, reading and music and music videos. Whether we grew up with all this type of exposure or not, it is ever present now, and we can learn to use the opportunities it affords. Professor Merzenich believes that these channels are tools for visualization, and they enable us to more easily visualize some outcome that might otherwise be unclear.

This visualization can be used to imagine success and what the positive outcomes may look like and also what are the options for positive results. Indeed our brains cannot tell the difference between visualization using our imagination and the real thing. Brain scans show that the same part of the brain is activated whether we close our eyes and imagine a daisy or whether we are looking at a daisy. So we can change our brains by imagining an act. Consequently practicing visualization can make things happen more readily; especially as the process of imagining uses brain muscles that are strengthened almost as much as if we actually do the exercise.

Professional golfers use visualization to imagine where their golf ball will land and have reported success with this technique. Prisoners of war have also used this technique to learn how to water-ski when incarcerated in prisons with no access to water or a boat. It is also used by health professionals to reduce the experience of pain as it was realized that visualization can affect our brains and diminish the pain experience. This, with practice and repetition, can be made into more permanent structures using our capacity for Neuroplasticity.

Both meditation and visualization are useful adjuncts to Breakthrough Training.

Control of Powerful Emotions

How can we control these emotions rather than let them to control us? According to Dr. Kevin Ochsner, who told his audience in his speech about managing emotions at a Neuro-Leadership Conference in New York City in October 2008, there are five major strategies to do so:-

- *Avoid repeated exposure to the situation*
- *Modify the circumstances*
- *Switch focus*
- *Reappraise or Re-interpret meanings*
- *Make adjustments to the response*

Strategy one: Avoid repeated exposure to the situation

- When overwhelmed we need to reduce our exposure to the thing or person who spurs this emotion; this could include not being around people who have the same fear as we do.
- Avoid repetitive reminders of the external dangers; this might mean switching TV channels or avoiding certain newspapers that chafe on that concern; it means being selective in what we read or watch.
- Deplete temptations; this may mean eliminating that item from our immediate environment; this could include not buying chocolate when we decide to go on a diet.
- Essential first step; while this may be a good short-term approach, it may be inadequate for longer term issues. Taking this first step allows us to move forward to other activities and strategies.

Strategy two: Modify the circumstances; get perspective.

- We can modify situation by bringing in less fear-inducing elements; this may mean that people who fear public speaking arrange to get to the hall early to practice.
- Get some mental breathing space; we can do this by physically distancing ourselves from the situation, and also by distancing ourselves mentally.
- Imagine the fearful event happened to someone else; this sounds uncharitable but it does give us a chance to practice our empathy skills.
- View it from a distance; this may mean that we are watching this stressful or fearful event from a great distance without judgment. This could be our perception from a plane at 30, 000 feet as we observe something impartially and without attachment.
- We can put a label on the action or on the event; we do this without feeling any emotional pull.
- We can think of events or successes we had in the past; often times when we successfully waited out the storm.
- We find alternate activities; this may include novel reading, going to the cinema, taking up meditation or painting.
- For balance; we need to ensure that we are looking after our needs for balanced nutrition and rest.

Strategy three: Switch focus

- Switch attention to something else; we can do this adjusting our focus and instead of being afraid of talking to a large group of people we focus on the wall behind a specific person.

- Identify the emotions we are feeling; using a label can assist the precise definition.

- Consider what provoked the feelings; we can think through similar situations and identify what triggered our emotive response.

- Maintain our impartiality; it helps if we can keep the items as impartial as possible without assigning a good or bad value.

- Select endpoints; we can review what we want to achieve and list some other ways to get there and what may be the easiest and most effective paths to take.

- Recognize this is our emotion; we acknowledge that we feel this way and no one has forced it on us, which puts us in the driver's seat to choose ways to be less fearful and stressed.

- Seek out effective alternatives; there are always different ways to get what we want and we can evaluate their merit.

- Reduce our emotional vulnerability; this can mean we maintain or re-establish a balanced approach to our nutrition and get adequate sleep and cut down on environmental stresses.

Strategy four: Re-appraise and Re-interpret

- Reappraise or reinterpret; this often means re-framing what has happened using more positive language and in a more upbeat way. This can be a powerful deterrent to depression, panic, and phobias.

- Focus on the longer term; if we have longer term fears about our financial situation we can shift our focus to a more distant future and imagine the next cyclical wave.
- Act it out; we can deploy our acting skills if faced by some action that normally would provoke an emotional response.

Strategy five: Make adjustments to the response-enhance the Positive

- Amend how we react; this means behaving in a different way, and perhaps might involve not showing our true emotional response.
- Be positive; as our brains cannot tell the difference between real and imagined happenings, we can emphasize the positives and adapt more positive self-talk.
- Move forward; we can consider alternate plans of action and then we adopt one to move forward and put it into place.
- Visualize; we imagine the situation and the outcome we want and this can help make it happen because our brains react the same way whether an event is real or imagined.
- Change our thinking; to do this involves a change to how we feel about something or someone and this will help change the outcome.
- "Best case" scenario; imagine the "best case" outcome we would like to see in the next year.
- Just do it; we can plan more pleasant and joyful activities now.

These strategies may not always be welcome since they represent ways of dealing with unpleasant or disagreeable emotions; moreover these strategies shake us out of tendencies to get set in our ways. They rely on addressing each emotion as a challenge for which we may find an alternative or a different way of behaving.

This, paradoxically, can be a path to positive Neuroplasticity and bring about renewal that sparks better focus, make more thoughtful decisions and boost our insightful perceptions, and keeps us on the path to Brain Fitness.

Making change sustainable

All changes in our brains are first treated as temporary switches but they can become permanent, using Neuroplasticity, with repetition over time; a process that is helped when stimulants are novel, and challenging.

The more we can control our emotions the more we are able to achieve personal equilibrium. With greater equilibrium we can incite increased balance of our core chemicals-notably dopamine and norepinephrine that actually provoke more BDNF and Neuroplasticity.

The five strategies can assist our abilities to re-assert control over our emotions so that we re-program our responses instead of reacting almost automatically to stress, or fear; both of which impede our brains by shutting down our abilities to grow new brain cells and Neuroplasticity. Moreover, the more we can re-program our feelings into more positive ones, the more we will be able to pre-empt our brains from adapting negative emotional responses that can become reinforced rigidities in our brains.

Paying Attention, Novelty and Challenge

There are a number of ways to stimulate our brains in Neuroplasticity, and the most important are physical and mental activities; these can become habits if we so choose.

Additionally it is vital to maintain focus by paying attention and ensuring that these ways offer challenges and novelty.

Neuroplasticity's impact on worries and stress

A good example of how we can use Neuroplasticity to diminish our worries and stress is set out in Jill Bolte Taylor's 2006 book, which outlines her type of stroke that paralyzed the left hemisphere of her brain, but which allowed her to concentrate more on the present moment and focus on relaxation. She opted to observe rather than engage, and was able to use her senses more fully, so that she could to pay attention to the environment, smell all the aromas and scents around her, listen carefully to all sounds, and be conscious of each movement of the body and how it feels.

In this way she is able to close down thinking stressful thoughts and maintain mastery over her emotions while she was undergoing rehabilitation to regain her physical motion. This illustrates how Breakthrough Training can help us direct our emotions, and how Neuroplasticity can solidify changes.

Summary

- Emotions are part of who we are, and there is no escaping them.
- They can hold a huge sway over us- but we always want to avoid letting them "Wag the dog".
- Strong Emotions --such as stress or fear, can become chronic and freeze our brains;
  - May deter Neuroplasticity, and can lead to brain power decline.
- Emotions are highly linked to our thoughts.
- Frozen feelings can lead to rigidity in thinking and inability to act or adapt.
- We can revive our brains flexibility and agility using the Five Strategies;
  - Avoid repeated exposure to the situation;
  - Modify circumstances;
  - Switch focus;
  - Reappraise or Re-interpret meanings;
  - Response modulation and enhance the Positive.
- As we regain mastery over our emotions we can make the changes more permanent using Neuroplasticity.
- This is one way to manage emotion; another uses Emotional Intelligence.
- Quiz

Brain Quiz No. 4: Inner Shape

Question—Is the inner shape a real circle?

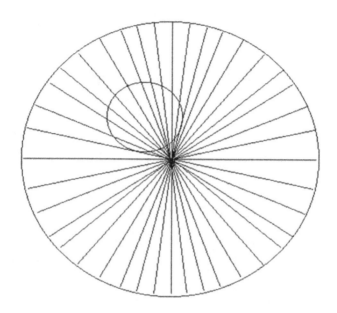

Answers are in Solutions at the end of the Book.

[Based on quiz at *www.SharpBrains.com*].

Chapter Five

Breakthrough Training— Emotional Intelligence

"Be like a duck, calm on the surface, but paddling like the dickens underneath"—Michael Caine

Another major aspect of Breakthrough Training

Breakthrough training is about understanding our thoughts and feelings and incorporating them into new patterns of behavior. This approach is reflective of today's paradigm that we seek out what works and what is effective. Breakthrough training incorporates developments in dialectical and cognitive behavioral dynamics that allow us to recognize our thoughts and feelings and use those techniques to alter them, as is appropriate. In addition to these two aspects of Breakthrough Training, the third string to the bow is Emotional Intelligence.

This is a growing field, and one which can help us get a valuable and special perspective on the Emotional Intelligence elements we truly need and gives us tools to enhance our comportment that advance our Brain Fitness.

Why is Emotional Intelligence relevant?

Emotional intelligence helps us understand ourselves and others better. It facilitates our knowledge of ourselves and how we manage ourselves, and it helps us make sense of the thoughts and feelings of other people and our abilities to build relationships and understand the actions of others.

In effect, it sets out a model path for us towards good personal self-knowledge, with good self control, and empathy and good relationships with others. The field has yielded some very useful tools from Emotional Intelligence work that can significantly boost our abilities for personal and social satisfaction and our chances of success, while at the same time we achieve our goals. Emotional Intelligence enables us to make changes that provide what we need for our circumstances to act more intelligently from all perspectives-including an emotional one. These changes can be imprinted into our brains using Neuroplasticity.

Emotional Intelligence

A number of people have lodged claims to be the originator of Emotional Intelligence. One widely published Harvard Business School professor, Daniel Goleman, has had a huge impact in making the concept more widely known. In one of his earlier works in 1998, he states that success in any field is highly linked to a person's emotional intelligence rather than general intelligence quotient; moreover " . . . how well you work has a lot to do with how well you discipline and motivate yourself." These are factors rely on major elements of Emotional Intelligence.

Other major contributors to this field include the work by Richard Boyatzis, whose 2007 work affirmed that people with high Emotional Intelligence have higher earning potential. Likewise motivational specialist, David McClelland, wrote in 2009 of a strong connection between achievement motivation and high levels of Emotional Intelligence.

Emotional Intelligence is now widely perceived as a major attribute of success that affects everything we do—even when we are alone; it will boost our confidence, morale and help us become more knowledgeable about ourselves as a pre-requisite for the next stage which is a better understanding of how to deal with others.

What is Emotional Intelligence?

The following Table indicates Emotional Intelligence has twenty elements that can be divided into four major aspects of our lives; these are:-

- Self-Awareness—understanding self;
- Self Management—ability to manage our emotions;
- Social Awareness—understanding others, social skills and empathy;
- Relationship Management—managing others and abilities to motivate.

Table 2: Elements of Emotional Intelligence -Major Categories

Self-Awareness	Social Awareness
Emotional self-awareness Accurate self assessment Self confidence	Empathy Organizational knowledge Service orientation
Self Management	**R e l a t i o n s h i p Management**
Emotional self-control Trustworthiness Conscientiousness Adaptability Achievement orientation Initiative	Influence Inspirational Leadership Developing others Building Bonds Teamwork & Collaboration Conflict management Communication Change Catalyst

Source: Nadler, Reldan (2006). Leader's Playbook.

Not all the twenty elements are vital to get a rating of high Emotional Intelligence. What we need, however, is to possess good rating in all four categories.

Emotionally Intelligent categories

I. Self-Awareness

High ratings in this category generally mean we know where we are headed and why. It includes the ability to imagine that we are standing outside ourselves and observe what we are feeling; we are able to define those emotions precisely and describe them with others. When we have high self-awareness we take personal responsibility for our emotions and thoughts, and do not lay the blame at someone else's door. Moreover, we recognize the importance of our feelings and those about others; we have an awareness of how this will affect our performance in any arena.

A core feeling in this category is empathy, or understanding where another person is coming from and how to interface effectively with that person.

- This self-knowledge is a vital component of our ability to pursue physical and mental exercise—necessary for Neuroplasticity; this category increases our assessment of what we need to provide for personal challenge and to bring in new elements.

Ways to boost Self-Awareness

Self Awareness is the cornerstone of getting to know where our thoughts come from and is one of the most important of all Emotional Intelligence skills. One effective way to improve this self-knowledge is to reflect at intervals throughout each day on:-

- What am I feeling right now?
- What do I want?
- How am I acting?
- What do my senses tell me?

Gradually with some practice this process gets faster and we are able to build self-confidence in what we are doing and in learning more about ourselves. We can re-shape how we look at our behaviors, and what we think and feel about them; all of which can be solidified by the action of Neuroplasticity.

Our destiny is not pre-determined simply by our DNA, but we have choices about what gets our full attention, how much and what types of physical and mental exercise we use to benefit from Brain Fitness. This building of self knowledge is an initial step from which we can build more Emotionally Intelligent attributes to take full responsibility for what we do and we are better able to mentor others.

II. Self Regulation and Managing Emotions

Mastery of this category frees us from being prisoner of our feelings. This requires finding ways to control our bad moods, or even lessen at times our exuberant moods. People who are in control of their feelings and impulses—are able to create an environment of trust and fairness. With training, this is something we are quite capable of doing; we can regulate our thoughts, emotions, and actions and plan ahead, resist distractions, and be goal-oriented by focusing our attention.

Also we are able to deal with fears, anxieties, anger without showing all our cards; this makes it easier for us to self-motivate to achieve our dreams by reducing the in-fighting and jealousies. It is as if we are having a private inner dialogue and although we may feel bad moods or certain impulses, we find ways to control them and even to channel them in useful ways. This may mean seeking out creative challenges, opportunities to learn, and enjoying a good job performance.

When we rate highly in this category we tend to have emotional self-control and are likely to be trustworthy, optimistic and we can self-motivate without reacting on impulse; we promote learning and are able to maintain emotional self-control that is not prone to counter-productive outbursts.

- When we have high ratings in the elements of this category we have abilities to overcome challenges. We can be successful in social engagements, seek tests and use our focus in physical and mental exercises rather than making them rote and unproductive sessions.

Ways to boost Self-Management

We can build our own assessment of how we perform as a self manager. Do we wear our emotions on our sleeves, or can we delay gratification and resist impulsive actions that are not well thought-through? One of the key ways is to assess our strengths and potential ways we can go off track.

Do we consider that following areas are strong points for us?

o   Emotional self-control;
o   Trustworthiness;
o   Conscientiousness;
o   Adaptability;
o   Achievement orientation;
o   Initiative.

We can give ourselves a star if we feel these are strong points and if on examination we are able to see how we can use them in the future in order to get an even better handle on managing our own personal feelings. Then we can review the list again, and select those areas that give us cause to reflect whether we could do this better; we can select one incident when our performance fell below what we know we could do better and then imagine how we would improve the way we acted.

III. Social Awareness

When we have a high ranking in Social Awareness we are effective at understanding how others feel and what they may be experiencing; this requires empathy on our part. We can understand our own feelings and the nature of our emotions, and can keep them under control. We can take an active interest in others, perceive their feelings and feel concern for them; additionally we can take their perspective and demonstrate empathy by showing we understand how they feel and why they act that way without necessarily endorsing those actions. In other words, we can walk a mile in their shoes without necessarily wanting them.

We also have a keen appreciation of how each group or organization functions, its power-plays and unwritten conventions. We may have excellent communication skills, which includes being able to listen actively or acutely, being good observers so that we notice body language and nuances of the spoken or unspoken word, and we are able to convey our messages succinctly-whether spoken or written.

- o This social awareness is a vital component of our ability to pursue social activities and engagements and have the comprehension necessary to make them challenging and novel and enjoyable.
- o We need this skill to be good at social engagement, which is one of the major stimulants for Neuroplasticity.
- o Also in the words of Dr. Joyce Brothers, when we have strong social awareness skills we tend to understand that "listening, not imitation, may be the sincerest form of flattery".

Ways to increasing Social Awareness and Empathy

Consider how well we:-

- o Understand other people;

- o Accurately hear unspoken words or partly expressed thoughts, feelings and concerns for others, and take active interest in other people's concerns;
- o Are self-aware and are able to pick up on feelings of others and recognize their emotions.

We can give ourselves a star if we feel that we do each of these things well and can justify the award to a highly demanding personal referee.

If there are areas that would beneficial for us to develop, we can highlight those and select one incident when we acted one way, but, as a socially aware person, we could have done something differently. We can imagine the action and how it would feel if we acted another way, and how we could adapt our personal repertoire in the future.

IV. Relationship Management

We are good at relationship management when we are adept at managing others; we have an ease at building rapport and we tend to be friendly and build bonds effectively and without effort. We have an aptitude to find common ground with others, and our communications contain clear messages with precise guidelines on ways to work well together.

We tend to have clear goals, approaches and expectations of the other person, and we are able to modulate our communication skills according to those required by the other person. We often are in a position to influence others, sometimes by providing inspiration and sometimes by acting as a change catalyst. The more we can control our own emotions and offer empathy, the more effective we will be good at managing relationships.

Some the tools for greater collaboration might include holding regular meetings, continual reviews and open door availability for feedback and comments, as well as the use of humor as a stress reliever and tension dissolver. This relies on trust and a sense of interdependency, and when we have high relationship management skills we take time to mentor others, keep motivation high, give timely feedback, and focus on the strengths of others.

- Core elements are developing others, communication and collaboration, and guiding others in friendly but persuasive ways. These are essential in social engagements and in building joint or team efforts in physical and mental exercises.

Ways to have more effective relationships

For the most part, we all are social beings and live in close proximity to others, and some of us may like that more than others, which may depend on our circumstances.

We may be married, have children, have families, have a work environment, work in a home office, and have many communities in which we participate. This aspect of Emotional Intelligence means that we run our relations with others in ways that are effective according to our perception.

This does not mean we dictate how others behave; nevertheless, we all have an influence on others—whether intentional or unintentional. We can ask ourselves:-

- Do we inspire others to follow a certain direction?
- Do we enable others to develop into who they truly are?
- Do we build connections with others?
- Do we cooperate with others?
- Do we handle disputes adeptly?
- Do we want to impose change?
- Are we clear about what we are doing and why, and communicate it effectively?

Would we give ourselves a golden star on all these issues? Even if we are doing well, there may always be ways to improve. In particular, consider two ways in which we can demonstrate:-

- Appreciation of the feelings and concerns of others;
- View of something from their perspective.
- Imagine how we can show empathy with the feelings of others, and understanding of why they act that way;
- Consider how we might modulate our response.

These are some of the core techniques of Emotional Intelligence and how we can build up what we need so that we are able to achieve Breakthrough Training and gain more control over our thoughts and emotions so that we can further our Brain Fitness.

Summary

- Breakthrough Training uses our Emotional Intelligence capabilities and enables us to leverage our whole brain.
- Enhancing our Emotional Intelligence is another way to master our thoughts, and feelings.
- The major components of Emotional Intelligence are:-
  o Self-Awareness—understanding self;
  o Self Management—ability to manage our emotions and understand self;
  o Social Awareness—understanding others, social skills and empathy;
  o Relationship Management—managing others and abilities to motivate.
- We can learn to enhance these components for Breakthrough Training.
- This aspect of Breakthrough Training enables us to act intelligently—in emotional and thinking ways.
- With the deployment of Neuroplasticity changes to our emotional responses will endure.
- Quiz.

Brain Quiz No. 5:-

Numbers game

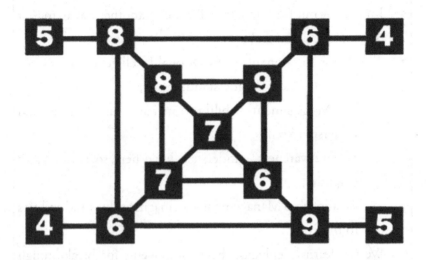

Start at the center number and collect another four numbers by following the paths shown (and not going backwards). Add the five numbers together. What is the lowest number you can score?

Answer at end of the Book.
[Based on Quiz at *www.SharpBrains.com*].

Part Three

Outlook for Brain Fitness-Effective Lessons and Prospects

Chapter Six

Ten Effective Ways to Boost Brain Fitness

"Life is what happens when you are making other plans".—John Lennon.

Effective Lessons to build Brain Fitness

Brain Fitness relies on certain fundamental requirements that will stimulate an increased production of BDNF to trigger Neuroplasticity. These core fundamental elements of Brain Fitness are derived from the actions stemming from Neurogenesis and Neuroplasticity; these notably include activities that stimulate greater production of BDNF and vital conditions.

Our future is not simply pre-determined by our genetic heritage, or DNA, but we can actively expand our range of feelings and thought patterns using Breakthrough Training techniques that will alter the ways we act. This will boost our ability to deploy Neuroplasticity and Breakthrough Training to make Brain Fitness changes that will stick.

Hence, we need Breakthrough Training to grow our brain-power and prevent any back-sliding as it enables us to have greater influence over our thought patterns and emotional responses. This promotes greater personal balance of feelings and thoughts as well as inner balance that affects our brain's chemical reactions and our moods. Moreover, working with the brain's Neuroplasticity, we can make these modified thought patterns and feelings more enduring.

These ten tools can help make Brain Fitness a reality, and are core elements for a new lifestyle, if we so choose. They are listed here in descending order but all make a major contribution to effective Brain Fitness.

1) Physical Exercise

This is the most important element in the creation of new neurons and the whole process of Neuroplasticity because exercise stimulates the additional production of Brain-Derived Neurotrophic Factor, BDNF more than any of the other nine factors.

It is not only good for our bodies but also empowers our minds to improve the functioning of our brains and enjoy the other benefits of Brain Fitness.

To be effective this exercise must last for at least thirty minutes and repeated at least five times a week. The physical exercise should include some aerobic or cardio-vascular training combined with balance and strengthening work. All forms of physical exercise need to have built-in challenges that test us in incremental steps.

The physical exercise can take many forms. It can be at a health club where machines and equipment are readily available. Appropriate types of physical exercise can include brisk walking or jogging outside, biking, and playing a sport.

There are also many exercises that help us attain more balance and flexibility. The practices of various forms of yoga are excellent ways to acquire more flexibility and balance. Moreover, Feldenkrais has the same type of effect as yoga but is a more western approach that combines physical exercise with mind development; it uses movement, both for our physical benefit and also as a means to increase our self-awareness so we are better able to perceive our array of choices and options to handle our emotions, relationships, and intellectual tasks more effectively.

2) Mental Activities

Similarly, mental activities require deliberate exercising. Our brains often prefer an "easy out," and may prefer to take the path of least resistance that is based on repeating past experience we have stored in our memory bank. Yet, when challenged our brains, even if inclined to be lazy, do thrive on new and demanding things to learn.

When we stimulate our brains through mental or intellectual challenges we force them to adapt to new environments and situations. Irrespective of our age, this propels Neurogenesis and it stimulates additional production of BDNF needed for Neuroplasticity.

Mental activities can take various forms; including learning to cha-cha, improving our Spanish or learning a new language, taking up juggling, learning to paint in oils or traveling. To be effective this activity should take at least 30 minutes and be repeated several times a week.

3) Social Activities

It is clear from all the studies and the various anecdotes we have heard that life in isolation does not allow us to exercise our minds and use our varied social, intellectual and relationship skills. It seems most likely that social interactions in any groups will allow us to develop and maintain our emotionally intelligent social awareness skills that stimulate our intellectual faculties and provide more impetus for our brains to use our Neuroplasticity.

These social interactions can take many forms and will vary according to our interests, our family situation and our preferences. It may give us opportunities to use or develop our humor, use our communication gifts to listening carefully or make speeches or enjoy the group dynamic. Such social interactions tend to be full of twists and surprises that keep our brains nimble and "fit".

4) Novelty, Challenge and Focus

Our brains respond to challenges, which may contain novel elements, and will demand our focus and attention. Indeed these factors are necessary for any change using our Neuroplastic abilities.

A physical exercise that is rote provides no challenge. Challenges can be heightened by bringing in new elements to consider; these novel, and possibly unexpected experiences, prompt our brain's machinery to switch gears in order to better master the new conditions. Both challenge and novelty are only effective if they are progressive, otherwise we give up and drop the activity.

Our brains are learning machines and to keep them strong we must continually extend our repertoire by discovering and mastering new things. We need to motivate these activities and make them rewarding and satisfying, since that amplifies our desire to expand our knowledge and memory using our Neuroplastic functions to solidify changes in our brains.

We can provoke challenge and newness in many ways; for instance, we can pursue new pastures by explorations and travel, which also require us to pay greater attention to our environment, and forces us to focus on new meanings of signs and language. We cannot make change without focus and by paying attention.

5) Transform Thought Patterns

Breakthrough Training enables us to manage our thoughts and emotional patterns that will spur Brain Fitness. This pioneering approach frees us from being prisoners of "same old story".

This aspect of Breakthrough Training is based on cognitive behavioral approaches to transforming our thought patterns and makes our thinking more explicit and open to learning and growth. The bulk of our thoughts are recycled from our past—indeed it is said that 95% of today's thoughts repeat those of yesterday. We can set ourselves free of this cycling mode by paying attention to what exactly are we thinking and how are we doing this.

Pure thinking is based on our perception of available data. This is significantly affected by what we want to achieve, or our goals. As the truism states, if we don't know where we are going then every road leads there. These techniques help us achieve our goals through deliberate and functional review of what and how we are thinking.

With practice we can build our knowledge of our thought patterns and take a proactive positive and future-oriented stance that, with Neuroplasticity, can become our default mindset so that we look forward to every new day in a constructive way.

In this way our thought patterns fit in with our overall strategies that reflect our goals. Via Breakthrough Training we will move consistently towards transformed thought patterns them and boost our Brain Fitness possibilities.

6) Taking care of Emotions

Breakthrough Training also deploys specific cognitive and dialectical behavioral techniques that enable us be better informed about our emotions and uncover ways to direct them.

We all have emotions and they are part of our personality. These emotions are a way of informing us whether that event is good or bad and are useful guides for what we like or dislike, or whom to trust or mistrust. Yet, at times, our emotions can become so powerful that they defy logic and we have a hard time coming to grips with them when they become powerful. Such strong emotions can include fear, anxiety or panic, stress or even love.

Taking care of our emotions is essential to Breakthrough Training, which provides us with behavioral techniques to direct our emotions, especially powerful ones. This will circumvent being sent off track and possibly sending us into a frozen or uncharacteristic mode of survival state that impedes the development of our abilities to trigger Neuroplasticity and reduces Brain Fitness.

The techniques help us better understand and ultimately direct our feelings in ways we prefer. This involves giving consideration to the underlying motivations and practice five core techniques that can help us take care of all our emotions for our greater well-being.

These strategies involve:-

- Avoidance of repeated exposure to the jarring event or situation that triggered the emotion;
- Change our perspective on the event or person that set off the emotion;
- Switch focus and attention away from the item that set off our emotion;
- Re-appraise or reinterpret the meanings of the event;
- Change the way we react.

7)   Emotional Intelligence

Breakthrough Training also includes Emotional Intelligence skills, which enable us to get a different perspective on our thoughts and emotional patterns and provides new elements to the Breakthrough Training toolbox to build what we need to be effective and behave in a sound balanced way.

These Emotional Intelligence tools can boost our self-knowledge, manage our reactions, enhance our empathy and understanding for others and help us develop more effective relationships. Using these tools we learn ways to expand our abilities and understand which elements could provide us with balance and equilibrium to attain our goals. With good self-knowledge and personal self-management we can get a better handle on our nature and preferences and learn how to leverage our strengths. Better understanding of other people enables smoother relationships and more socialization.

With the assistance of these Breakthrough Training tools we can establish appreciably more control over our emotions, and thought patterns, and the resultant equilibrium allows more chemical stability in our brains that will facilitate Neuroplasticity and consequent Brain Fitness.

8)   Do not Outsource our Brain-Power

We all are faced with the temptation to reiterate the views expressed by some pundits on TV or in the Press about a political event or personality. These people are paid to have opinions and sometimes we are inclined to adopt theirs without sufficient review. When we do this we are in effect just "outsourcing" our ideas, which do not promote our own brain power, nor do they challenge us in any way to come up with our own new or consolidated views.

Unfortunately the media is resorting more and more to the use of these so-called "experts", but that does not mean we have to accept their views on sports plays, sports persons, media personalities, politicians and the like.

We need to make our own decisions, and our own mistakes. Failure to do so can reduce our ability to learn from our mistakes, and negate our efforts to train our Brains for our benefit. We can improve these odds through the use of our own intellectual faculties so that we forge our own reasoned opinions.

9)　Meditation and Visualization

Meditation enables us to get in touch with our feelings; both negative and positive and can introduce us to more balance. There are various modes of meditation, and they all help quieten the mind, and can focus our minds to greater attentional stability; moreover meditation can reduce the impact of strong negative emotions by reversing the constraining effect of stress or fear on progress towards Neuroplasticity and Brain Fitness.

Sculpture by Henry Moore—on loan to Kew Gardens, UK.

Visualization also produces positive effects for boosting Brain Fitness. Our brains cannot tell the difference between visualization using our imagination and the real thing. Since the process of imagining uses brain muscles that are strengthened almost as much as when we actually do the exercise. Hence, if we imagine Y and it is something that can reinforce a basic message, then we are able to change our brains and boost the use of Neuroplasticity and Brain Fitness.

10) Balanced Nutrition and "Self-Care"

Nutrition

Looking after ourselves, what we put in our bodies and how much we are exposed to environmental stress, or even internal stress, has a huge impact of the chemical workings of our brains; and as a consequence it impacts our abilities to effectively pursue Brain Fitness.

Balanced nutrition means we consume proteins, carbohydrates and fats in a proportionate way to our physical needs. This basically simple idea is complicated by marketing strategies of food companies and supermarkets and the joys of modern food processing and is further compounded by the speed and nature of our lives.

When we get off balance, we consume disproportionate amounts of sugars and carbohydrates that can cause increased insulin levels, which in turn can mean we store more body fat and we experience a drop in our blood sugar concentration; this starves the brain and causes us to feel hungrier. Poor nutrition is no friend of Brain Fitness.

Tending to our nutrition does not imply diets that can cause weight fluctuations, nor does it mean deprivation that may be associated with punishment. An effective approach to a balanced nutrition is the "Zone" approach that encourages us to stimulate more Neuroplasticity by paying attention to what we eat and put into our bodies.

Self-Care

The more we use Breakthrough Training to enhance our Brain Fitness using the Brain's plasticity, the more we realize that we can only move forward if we know more about ourselves and can take care of ourselves to avoid potential pitfalls.

This means we can use emotionally intelligent tools to get clear about our preferences and how we can hold them in check. This assists us with recognizing our own boundaries and those of other people, which might boost our capacity for empathy.

Part of who we are depends on the values and beliefs that are important in our lives. These will reflect our original culture; this, as described by Geert Hofstede (2001) and by Fons Trompenaars and Charles Hampden-Turner (1998), will establish our cultural priorities and preferences. While these will differ around the world, we do need to be flexible and accept that differences in emphasis will persist and we have to accept the ambiguity rather than feel any personal threat.

In our social interactions, a major factor that can lead to disruptions is just how much we reveal to others about ourselves. This will depend on our circumstances. It is an opportunity to deploy Breakthrough Training's Emotional Intelligence skills so that we assess the relationship and use our influence wisely rather than disturb our path to Neuroplasticity and Brain Fitness.

Boosting effective Brain Fitness needs all these elements; some are fundamental to maintain Neurogenesis and stimulate Neuroplasticity, and others, notably the Breakthrough Training tools are vital to maintain forward impetus to our Brain Fitness.

We can choose whether we covert these lessons into habits, and, if so, we are on our way to make Brain Fitness our new lifestyle.

Summary

There are ten effective ways to boost our Brain Fitness.

Some are fundamental requirements for Neuroplasticity and Brain Fitness.

- Crucial ones stimulate the production of BDNF for Neuroplasticity;
  - Deliberate Physical exercise;
  - Purposeful mental exercise and social engagement;
  - Ensuring all these factors are challenging, novel and demand full attention.

The other seven lessons are based on aspects of Breakthrough Training and are essential to develop effective Brain Fitness. These are:-

- Transforming thought patterns;
- Taking care of emotions;
- Enhance breakthrough training-using emotional intelligence techniques;
- Do not outsource your brain;
- Meditation and Visualization;
- Balanced Nutrition and Self-Care.

These can become ways we can make Brain Fitness part of our Lifestyle

- Quiz

Brain Quiz No. 6:

Mental Gymnastics and Imagination

1. Recite the days of the week in reverse alphabetical order.
2. Recite the months of the year in alphabetical order.
3. Calculate the sum of your date of birth, using mm/dd/yyyy.
4. Look around and within two minutes, find 5 red things that will fit in your pocket, and 5 blue objects that are too big to fit.

Solutions are at the end of the Book.

[Based on quiz at *www.SharpBrains.com*].

Chapter Seven

Prospects for Brain Fitness and Breakthrough Training for Those Who Mind

"All would live long, but none would be old".—Benjamin Franklin

This is a journey across the frontiers of modern thinking in which we explore how our brains function, how we can boost their strength and resilience, and in what ways can we best master our reactions and take back our power over our thoughts, emotion and actions in order to boost Neuroplasticity and our consequent levels of Brain Fitness to our advantage.

Future and Prospects of Brain Fitness

Brain Fitness is emerging as a promising new approach that offers enormous benefits. It is evident that in the future, more and more people will come to appreciate the importance of Brain Fitness.

This is especially true, as we are likely to live longer lives and we would like our mental prowess to accompany our life-span. Starting early means our brains will be better connected, more resilient and stronger, and so better able to resist decline longer. Indeed, some research indicates that we can build up our Brain Fitness reserves for future use to deflect future or even budding impairments.

What will Brain Fitness look like down the road? Here are seven predictions:-

i. Progressively, as the benefits of Brain Fitness become better known, greater numbers of people from different walks of life, and different age groups, will seek out Brain Fitness programs. Supported by new data from research, Brain Fitness programs will expand their appeal to incorporate a wider audience span.

ii. More programs will be offered by more health clubs, country clubs, and corporate wellness programs as well as on the Internet. Access will be easier—both for the user and provider of Brain Fitness programs; this is good news, although some caution is advised as not all programs will get it right.

iii. Breakthrough Training provides a do-it-yourself guide that outlines core strategies; these can be complemented with novel and challenging tactics suggested on the Internet or at a club.

iv. Brain Fitness has obvious benefits and it can become easily be incorporated into our modern and more enlightened lifestyle; especially as technology will one day provides us with lightweight gadgets that calculate our progress to Brain Fitness.

v.   To circumvent abuse, there will be specialized training with certifications.

vi.   As interest mounts, there will be increased research into Brain Fitness; this will notably focus on the reserve capacity notion and to ward off Alzheimer's and on the impact of Brain Fitness for young people.

vii.   Programs will become more integrated or more readily available so that we will be able to fulfill the requirements for Brain Fitness more easily with more one-stop "shopping".

Brain Quiz No. 7: Whole Brain Puzzle

A blind beggar had a brother who died.
What relation was the blind beggar to the brother who died?

Answer in Solutions at end of Book.
[Based on Quiz at *www.SharpBrains.com*].

Advantages of Breakthrough Training

Breakthrough Training offers significant rewards. It enables us to weave our way through complicated cognitive and emotional scenarios, so that we are better positioned to manage our lives in ways that help us benefit more fully from Brain Fitness. It will assist us overcome hurdles, and give us clear strategies to follow.

Here are some of the ways we can profit from Breakthrough Training to boost our Brain Fitness:-

Breakthrough Training

Breakthrough Training gives us techniques that let us to better address our ways of thinking and feeling in order to direct our moods. The interactions are complex, but with Breakthrough Training we can sever the vicious circle that often entraps us, so that we have more control over our thoughts and feelings that determine our brain's levels of Dopamine and Norepinephrine, which not only influence our feelings, thoughts and behaviors, but also stimulate additional production in the brain of the chemical, BDNF, which we need for Neuroplasticity and all its benefits.

This Breakthrough Training consists of several approaches. We can use Dialectical and Cognitive processes to facilitate greater understanding of the nature of our thoughts and our emotions. These techniques are valuable building blocks that can help us alter or modify our rational or emotive reactions to fit the current situation and circumstances. These techniques that are part of Breakthrough Training and facilitate change.

Another equally fruitful approach deployed by Breakthrough Training, is to use of our Emotional Intelligence skills; this enables us to take a different perspective over our cognitive abilities, and modify the necessary ones to succeed in achieving our aims.

Emotional Intelligence has twenty elements that are usually broken down into four major categories. We do not need all these mechanisms, but we do need to ensure that we have adequate levels in all four categories. These fortunately are all learnable at any age.

In addition Breakthrough Training also includes techniques that use meditation, visualization and self-care. With this wide palette of actions, Breakthrough Training can facilitate actions to boost our confidence, be more willing to tackle challenges, build deeper relationships, reduce and manage stress and gain greater control over our thoughts and feelings. It enables us to boost our levels of Brain Fitness and its effective use.

This in combination with the actions of Neuroplasticity will make changes to our thoughts and emotional patterns more enduring.

Wisdom of Age

Getting older is unavoidable but falling apart is not. We all age, but that doesn't mean that inevitably our bodies and minds will go to wrack and ruin.

We have a choice; we can use techniques of Breakthrough Training that will improve the way our brains function, allows us more mastery over our thoughts and emotions, and this increased balance complements and feeds into Neurogenesis and Neuroplasticity processes that can make changes more enduring and also slow, or in some cases, reverse the normal aging process and boost our repair and maintenance options.

As science has advanced, we have learned more about how our Brains work. The technological advances permit us to see the chemicals released and how they affect our Brain's ability to grow and re-wire itself. Indeed, as Michael Merzenich says " . . . our brains were created to reinvent and reconfigure themselves throughout our lifetimes".

So we can build in more compensation for age's effects by using Breakthrough Training, combined with our brain's plasticity, and with more practice we can accelerate the rate of change that brings improved processing speed, better memory, more focus and where appropriate aid compensatory measures for injury and disease.

Three major Stimulants

Breakthrough Training affects our progress towards balanced cognitive functions that is vital for Brain Fitness. Yet, we cannot progress to Brain Fitness without Neurogenesis to permit the brain to prompt the growth of new nerve cells, and the crucial process of Neuroplasticity that must be stimulated into action. These major stimulants are Physical and Mental Exercise and Socialization.

Each of these factors must be undertaken deliberately, and with clear intention and focus on what we strive to achieve; moreover these stimulants must present a challenge and incremental demands on our faculties. Breakthrough Training can boost our abilities as it gives us greater emotional and cognitive control that will support our ability to pay attention in finding resolutions to the dilemmas raised by these stimulating factors.

Reserve Capacity

There is some recent evidence from research lead by Dr. David Bennett at Rush University in Chicago, which indicates that through Brain Fitness we can generate surplus reserve capacities with their new connections and pathways; this we can use later in our lives. The work of the team in Chicago postulates that stimulating activities over and above those needed for current requirements, can build a mental reserve capacity that can modulate brain damage by warding off the development of Alzheimer's disease.

Dr Bennett's study tracked some 2000 people over several years. After the deaths of two-thirds of the population, the researchers determined that none had an Alzheimer's diagnosis or even suffered mild cognitive decline, even though one third of that deceased population had some symptoms, such as, the tangles and plaques of Alzheimer's. The explanation, according to this study, is that these people had sufficient reserve capacity of Brain Fitness to exhibit good thinking skills and showed no clinical signs of the Alzheimer's illness. Moreover Dr. Bennett believes this supports the "use it or lose it" doctrine.

This has huge potential, and is the subject of considerable further research. It is possible that this reserve capacity operates like a mental savings account that we can draw on when needed, and it argues in favor of continuously building our Brain Fitness, not only for the current benefits, but also as a form of insurance against future dangers of mental decline.

Staying Sharp

Brain Fitness is a major strategy to help our minds stay sharp. Work by Bridget Kuehn in 2006 demonstrated that Brain Fitness does have that effect. Her study found that Neuroplasticity, with it increased production of BDNF, and which was stimulated by physical, mental exercise and socialization, promoted faster thinking, improved memory and language skills and clearer decision-making. These are all elements that are vital for our independence and maintaining the sharpness of our brain's functions.

Purpose and Quality of life

Using Breakthrough Training and Neuroplasticity we can boost our level of Brain Fitness that brings so many benefits to our lives. It dramatically increases the probability of staying mentally and physically fit throughout our lives, which translates directly into improved quality of our lives and providing more fulfilling experiences.

Brain Fitness also contributes to a feeling of full involvement and energized focus or "Flow". This concept of Flow was identified by psychologist, Mihaly Csikszentmihalyi, many years ago in 1990. Csikszentmihalyi describes this "Flow" state as one of being fully absorbed by novel situations and by dealing with grand challenges that require motivation and focused attention.

This is similar to the conditions that can trigger Neuroplasticity, and clearly Brain Fitness can also prompt something similar to the "Flow" state that has been shown to improve our experience of joy and happiness and improved quality of life. That is important as there is little point in gaining all the benefits of Brain Fitness if we lack quality to our lives.

Moreover that quality needs to have in-built purpose. A study by D. Buettner in AARP magazine in 2008, demonstrated that people who lead purposeful and quality lives, suffer fewer incidents of disease. Buettner's study of 13,000 middle-age people in Hungary found that those with meaning to their lives had lower rates of cancer and heart disease than those who did not have as much purpose and meaning.

In the words of Deepak Chopra (2008), "purpose gives you fulfillment and joy, and that can bring the experience of happiness".

How do we know we have found our purpose?

We have all had some form of peak experience. It may have been the time when we were congratulated at school for our excellent table tennis performance, or when our favorite baseball team wins the pennant. One way to re-experience that quality and peak experience is to use our imagination and visualization skills to re-visit that time when things went extremely well, and remember how we felt during these peak experiences.

Effective Brain Fitness—a Win-Win opportunity

Henry Moore's Sculpture—in Kew Gardens, UK.

Brain Fitness can help us live life to the full. It is about being a better person; it helps us lead more fascinating and interesting lives and take an interest in what is going on around us. Rather than seeking comforts we can seek out challenges and new things to tackle.

Breakthrough Training, combined with the malleability of our brains, offers a useful recipe to take back more control over our memory and accuracy of our recall, our problem solving and decision-making abilities, our empathy and boost our savoir-faire and our personal satisfaction. These qualitative and quantitative aspects can give us, in the words of Michael Merzenich in the 2007 PBS program on Brain Fitness, the chance that our brain span will eclipse our life span.

Summary

- Brain Fitness is a promising new approach.
  - It has excellent prospects for a wider audience, more certifications of trainers and a new way of life.

- Breakthrough Training's pioneering approach will boost effective use of Brain Fitness.
- Brain Fitness allows us to feel more wisdom.
- With genuine benefits, Brain Fitness can become our new Lifestyle
- This is a strategic plan for a do-it-yourself Brain Fitness program.
- This program can bring joy and mental dancing, confidence, spark and revive our "savoir-faire".

- Enjoy.

Brain Quiz No. 8:

Leaves in the Amazon vs. Connections in our Brains

Are there more connections in our Brain than leaves in the Rain Forest in the Amazon?

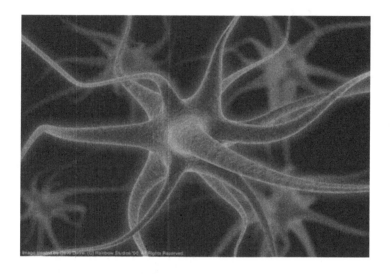

Solution is in the next section.
[Based on a quiz at *www.SharpBrains.com*].

Solutions to Quizzes

Quiz No. 1—Tipping the Scales

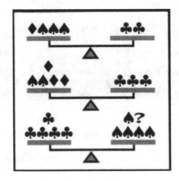

Question:—The top two scales are in perfect balance. How many diamonds will be needed to balance the bottom set?

The answer is—Four diamonds

[First add up the number of Clubs in the first two scales =5. Then count the number of Clubs in the bottom scale =5. Then do the same with the Spades, which equals 5 and

5. There are 4 diamonds in the top two balanced scales. Therefore, it must take 4 diamonds to balance the third scale since all the other measurements are the same].

Quiz No. 2—Find third word associated with both these words:-

- PIANO—LOCK > Key
- SHIP—CARD > Deck
- TREE—CAR > Trunk
- SCHOOL—EYE > Pupil (Exam and Private are also possible)
- PILLOW—COURT > Case
- RIVER—MONEY > Bank (Flow is also possible)
- BED—PAPER > Sheet
- ARMY—WATER > Tank
- TENNIS—NOISE > Racket
- EGYPTIAN—MOTHER > Mummy
- SMOKER—PLUMBER > Pipe

Quiz No. 3—Memory and Thinking skills

Questions are:-

- Name the one sport in which neither spectators nor participants know the score until the contest ends.
- What famous North American landmark is constantly moving backward?
- Only two vegetables can produce for several growing seasons-all others are annuals. What are they?
- What fruit has its seeds on the outside?

- Name the one vegetable or fruit that is never sold frozen, canned, processed, or cooked.
- Name 5 things that you can wear on your feet beginning with the letter "S."

Answers are:-

- Boxing
- Niagara Falls
- Asparagus and Rhubarb
- Strawberry
- Lettuce
- Shoes, socks, sandals, sneakers, skis, skates, snowshoes, stocking, stilts, surfboard.

Quiz No. 4-Inner shape

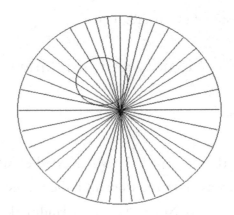

Question:—Is the inner shape a real circle?

Answer:—Both shapes are perfect circles.

Quiz No. 5: Numbers quiz

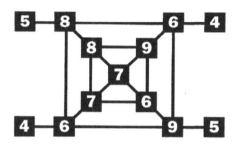

Question:—

Start at the center number and collect another four numbers by following the paths shown (and not going backwards). Add the five numbers together. What is the lowest number you can score?

The Answer is 30

Quiz No. 6:—Mental Gymnastics and Imagination

Questions:

1. Recite the days of the week in reverse alphabetical order.
2. Recite the months of the year in alphabetical order.
3. Calculate the sum of your date of birth, using mm/dd/yyyy.
4. Look around and within two minutes, find 5 red things that will fit in your pocket, and 5 blue objects that are too big to fit.

Answers are:-

- Wednesday, Tuesday, Thursday, Sunday, Saturday, Monday, Friday

- April, August, February, December, January, July, June, March, May, November, October, September.
- E.g. Author's =30
- Optional weekend activity—Look around and within two minutes; find 5 red things that will fit in your pocket, and 5 blue objects that are too big to fit.

Quiz No. 7—Whole Brain Puzzle

Question:—

A blind beggar had a brother who died. What relation was the blind beggar to the brother who died?

Answer:—The blind beggar was the *sister* of her brother, who died.

Quiz No. 8: Leaves in Amazon

Question:—Are there more Connections in our Brains than Leaves in the Amazon?

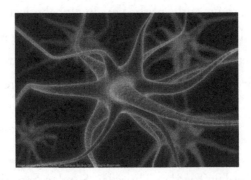

Answer: About the same number—circa 1000 trillion.

Bibliography

Begley, Sharon, (2007). "Train your Mind, Change your Brain". Ballantine Books. New York, NY.

Bennett, D. A., Schneider, J.A., Tang, Y., Arnold, S.E. The Effect of Social Networks on the Relation between Alzheimer's Disease Pathology . . . "Lancet Neurology", 2006 published by Elsevier.

Brown, Arnold. The Biology Paradigm. "The Futurist". September-October 2008, published by World Future Society.

Buettner, D. Find Purpose, Live Longer. "AARP Magazine". November/December, 2008.

Boyatzis, R.E. (2007). Mentoring for Intentional Behavior Change. In "The Handbook of Mentoring". Ragins & Kram (Eds.). Erlbaum Publishers.

Brain Teasers. Retrieved on February 14, 2009 from *www.sharpbrains. com*.

Carr, J. E., & LeBlanc, L. A. (2003). Functional analysis of problem behavior. In W. O'Donohue, J. E. Fisher, & S. C. Hayes (Eds.), "Cognitive behavior therapy: Applying empirically supported techniques in your practice" (pp. 167-175). Wiley, Hoboken, NJ.

Cassel, C.K. Use it or lose it. "Journal of the American Medical Association" (JAMA). Vol. 288 No. 18, November 13, 2002

Chopra, D. (2008). "Ageless Body, Timeless Mind: A Practical Alternative to Growing Old". Rider, Ebury Publishing. New York City; NY.

Csikszentmihalyi, Mihaly. (1990). "Flow". Harper & Row; New York City, NY.

Doraiswamy, P.M., Gwyther, L., Adler, T. The Alzheimer Action Plan: The Expert's Guide to the Best Diagnosis and Treatment for Memory Problems. "Journal of the American Medical Association", (JAMA). Vol. 300 No. 3, July 16, 2008.

Doidge, Norman. (2007). "The Brain That Changes Itself: Stories of Personal Triumph from the Frontiers of Brain Science". Penguin Group, NYC, NY.

Alvaro Fernandez Top Ten Brain Training Future Trends. Retrieved from *www.sharpbrains.com* on October 30, 2008.

Friedrich, M.J. Exercise May Boost Aging Immune system. "Journal of the American Medical Association", (JAMA). Vol. 299 No. 2, January 9-16, 2008.

Linehan, M. M. (1993). "Cognitive Behavioral Treatment of Borderline Personality Disorders". Guilford Press, NYC, NY.

Gottfurcht, James. Retrieved from *www.PyschologyofMoney.com* on February 21, 2009.

Goldberg, E. (2007). "The Wisdom Paradox: How Your Mind Can Grow Stronger As Your Brain Grows Older". Pocket Books. NYC, NY.

Hofstede, Geert. (2001). "Culture's consequences: Comparing values, behaviors, institutions, and organizations across nations". 2nd Ed. Thousand Oaks CA: Sage Publications.

Kuehn, Bridget "Strategies for staying sharp". "Journal of the American Medical Association", (JAMA). Vol. 295; No. 5; February 1, 2006.

Kuhn, Thomas, S., (1962). "The Structure of Scientific Revolutions". The University of Chicago Press, Chicago, Ill.

McClelland, D. (2009). Employee Motivation, the Organizational Environment and Productivity. Retrieved from *www.accelteam.com/human_relations/hrels_06* on February 16, 2009.

Miller, Michael Craig, M.D., Health for Life: Sad Brain, Happy Brain. "Newsweek", September 22, 2008.

Mitka, M. Aging Patients are advised "Stay Active to Stay Alert". "Journal of the American Medical Association", (JAMA). Vol. 285, No. 19, May 16, 2001

Nadler, Reldan S. (2006) "Leaders Playbook". Psyccess Press; Santa Barbara: CA.

National Institutes of Health. Retrieved on December 20, 2008. *www.pubs.niaaa.nih.gov/publications/arh23-2/078-85.pdf.*

National Institutes of Health (N.I.H). Stress System Malfunction could lead to serious Life-Threatening Diseases. "NIH Backgrounder". September 9, 2002.

Ochsner, Kevin. The Science of Managing Fears. "Neuro-Leadership Conference"—New York City, New York. October 29, 2008

PBS Home Video, (2008). "The Brain Fitness Program". Santa Fe Productions Inc. UBRN601. PBS.

Polya, A. J. (2008). Playing your strengths. The Polya Group Newsletter:—Vol. 5 No.1 January-March 2008. Retrieved from *http://ThePolyaGroup.com* on February 14, 2009.

Price, Jill, and Davis, B. (2008). "The Woman who cannot forget: The extraordinary story of living with the most remarkable memory known to science". NYC; NY.

Ratey, John, and Hagerman, E. (2008). "Spark: The Revolutionary New Science of Exercise and the Brain". Little Brown & Co. NY, NY.

Rath, Tom, (2007). "Strengths Finder—2.0". The Gallup Organization. New York, NY.

Rueda, M.R., Posner, M.I., and Rothbart, M.K. (2005). The development of executive attention: contributions to the emergence of self regulation. "Developmental NeuroPsychology".

Schweitzer, M & Gino, F. Feeling the Love (or Anger): How Emotions Can Distort the Way We Respond to Advice". Retrieved on October 29, 2008 from *www.knowledge@Wharton.edu*

Seligman, Martin, and Csikszentmihalyi, Mihaly. Retrieved on October 18, 2008 from *www.authentichappiness.org*

Taub, E., Uswatte, G., King, D.K., Morris, D., Crago, J.E. and Chatterjee, A. Placebo-Controlled Trials of Constraint-Induced Movement Therapy for Upper Extremity after Stroke. "Stroke". April, 2006.

Tang, Y., Ma, Y., Wang, J., Fan, Y., Feng, S., Lu, Q., and et al. (2007). Short-term Meditation Training Improves Attention and Self-Regulation. Proceedings of the "National Academy of Sciences". 104(43), 17152-17156.

Taylor, J.B. (2006). "My Stroke of Insight: A Brain Scientist's Personal Journey". Viking Press, NYC, NY.

Trompenaars, Fons and Hampden Turner, Charles.(1998). "Riding the Waves of Culture: understanding diversity in global business". New York City, NY: McGraw-Hill.

Rueda, M. R., Rothbart, M. K. & Saccamanno, L. & Posner, M.I. Training, Maturation and Genetic Influences on the Development of

Executive Attention. "Proceedings at the U.S National Academy of Sciences". (2005); Vol. 102.

Rueda, M.R., Posner, M.I., & Rothbart, M.K. (2005). The Development of Executive Attention: Contributions to the Emergence of Self Regulation. "Developmental Neuro-Psychology". Vol.28, 573-594.

Zak, P.J. Mind over Money. "Monitor on Psychology". January, 2009; Vol. 40(1).

Tables

Table One:

Behavioral Chain. Based on work by Linehan, M. M. (1993) and Carr, J. E., & LeBlanc, L. A. (2003), adapted and modified by Ann J. Polya, Ph.D. (2009).

Table Two:

Elements of Emotional Intelligence-Major Categories. Source—Nadler, Reldan (2006). "Leader's Playbook".